Finding Trout

By Tony Ritchie

Published and distributed by
Australian Fishing Network
48 Centre Way, Croydon South, Victoria 3136
Telephone (03) 9761 4044 Fax (03) 9761 4055
Email: sales@afn.com.au
Website: www.afn.com.au

ISBN 1 86513 064 8

Contents

Preface

The aim of this book is to help the sporting angler find trout to catch. Its theory is based largely on the trout itself, especially the brown trout whose consistent traits can demoralise or, when correctly understood in conjunction with external influences, reward with wonderful satisfaction. Its practice has been conducted for the most part in Australia's island state, Tasmania, and to a certain extent is biased: mainly towards fishing to moving trout, partly towards the use of the fly by a wading angler on moving water.

Even though the detailed examples are based largely on trout waters in Tasmania, I do feel, however, that its principles are broad enough to make this book of value to anglers elsewhere using any sporting method to attract any of the various species of trout.

Inherent in angling are many variables whose relative importance changes from place to place and if not from hour to hour, certainly from one day to the next. They are intertwined with each other and with the how, what and when of the sport. Anglers could go on learning about them forever, which is an important reason in itself to continue to do just that.

I hope, nevertheless, you agree with me that there are generalisations which I can usefully make right now, even though any angler of some experience knows full well that each of them, and probably sooner rather than later, will be built upon and modified as knowledge increases. This publication, expanded and upgraded from my previous *Finding Feeding Trout*, is itself an example.

I hope also that you will gain fresh insights into why our speckled admission tickets behave as they do, and that through enjoying your participation in Nature's show you are inspired to ensure that it continues.

Acknowledgments

As well as the people mentioned in the text and bibliography, I thank many others who have been kind enough to offer valuable insights into why trout feed where they do.
These include Messrs S. Chilcott, P. Cunningham, K. Fletcher, N. Forteath, G. French, D. Gilmour, M. Heazlewood, T. Kelly. O. Kehrberg, R. Klimeck, F. Lunstroo, A. Miller, C. Peck, L. Ritchie, P.J. Ritchie, A. Shepherd, E. and L. Smith, V. Spencer, B. Thompson and J. Wedd. Also much appreciated is the help given by David Scholes, specifically for furnishing vital percepts on trout vision and flood fishing.

Lake St Clair Lagoon, where an out-flowing current carries food to waiting trout — and where the backdrop can distract an angler …

Chapter 1
Trout Food - Drift

There I was on a pleasant afternoon in midspring, idly wandering with a fishing friend along a northern Tasmanian river meandering slowly and quietly over its wide floodplain. Flanked by associated sidewaters, the South Esk typified many other Australian streams in trout country-a 'flat' river which today sadly matched our flat spirits.

We had been hoping for mayfly sport, but although the day seemed warm enough, no flies of any kind could we see, and no trout moved along the river, swollen for a week now and still running a banker. Barren also were its main sidewaters, backwaters and billabongs, usually dependable if prospected long enough-and that Ray and I had already tried, flogging wet and dry flies for hours for not one swirl.

In desperation I tried unlikely water: the head of a small sidestream that ran only in times of flood out of a large, weedy basin and down all by itself through a few paddocks to rejoin the river a kilometre below. I was surprised when a fish boiled near its outlet at my wet fly. Yet that was the only sign of interest, and we mumbled to each other about summers and single swallows.

Time to try somewhere else? What was this little stream like farther down, though? We jumped into the jeep and drove along the fenceline to where we knew it dog-legged left-a simple enough inspection, but one we'd never bothered with in the past.

'There's no fool like an old fool', I observed sadly to Ray, after a few minutes' easy drive through the rolling, open paddock had brought us to a low bank above a weedy, straight watercourse. 'Why didn't I ever look in all those other floods?'

A trout swirled in front of us as I spoke, so we unlimbered the rods without delay. Even though it was too weedy for metal lures, fish here would probably have taken bait such as worms properly

presented but for us on went small dry flies.

Ray let his size 14 Pheasant Tail Dun float down over a swirl, was into a trout first go and followed that with another a few casts later. They were chunky, strong browns of between 0.5 and 1 kg, and Ray drifted off downstream looking for bigger ones.

I headed back up, coming upon several narrow, faster runs where two fish were cruising resolutely

Great Lake at sunset, when drifting food accumulates at the edge of the slick.

but without pattern, sometimes swirling, sometimes surging, both plainly feeding well. One took offence probably at my line in the air and sped off downstream, while the other went on touring unpredictably-above my Brown Dun one minute, below it the next. But then the fish steamed casually upstream, on the way clipping my little

Ray was into a trout first go.

Playing it. 'How far out can I wa

floater down seemingly as an afterthought.

I lifted the rod immediately, immediately the battle began-and what a battle it proved to be!

This trout was obviously a very good one, but in such shallow water it could but run, or go for weed. Luckily, it chose to run-and so therefore must I, blundering and splashing through tall, drowned tussocks with one eye on the fish and the other on the waterweeds. Through them my leader was now tracing a sudden, jagged course, with a noise like a breeze among the willows that would fall for a moment to a whisper only to swell again as the fish took fright afresh.

Down we went for an eternity I later estimated to be 100 metres, with me hoping along the way that several muscular cylindrical shapes which writhed

briefly underfoot were eels. After dashing from one side to the other, there the big brown decided at last to sulk in weed. But its timing was wrong and to net it came without much more ado, those earlier frantic sprints pulling my line through such heavy weed taking their toll.

At 1.7 kg, or nearly 4 pounds, it was a beautifully-shaped trout in superb condition. I shook my head after photographing it, and again wondered just how I'd managed to steer clear of river trout like this one for so many years.

After coming unstuck from another strong fish, Ray had pushed up to rejoin me. Together we stood and marvelled at half a dozen trout, darting busily here and there over gravelly shallows, just below the knotted surface and practically under the tips of

Chunky, strong browns... 'About time, too.'

Playing another a few casts later.

our rods. I suspected drifting snails, thinking of past high, warm flows over such weed.

Snails or not, one of these fish soon noticed Ray's Dun, took confidently as it likely would have taken a worm or tiny metal lure … and another fight was on.

This trout thought about its battle plan for a time, surging up in the fast flow only to drift back again as it did so. Then off it lit for slow water along the far edge, but finding pressure still on its jaw there, dashed back almost to Ray's feet, to flounder about in a shin-deep basin among the tussocks and sheltered by two little hawthorns.

To and fro it rushed again, across the currents and back, with Ray contorting himself to stay in touch: sometimes with the quivering rod tip

properly overhead but at other times having it arched in strange directions behind his chest, or waist.

Probably unable below the ruffled surface to fix its opponent, the trout finally seemed to lose inspiration and fell back to surging up and down again in midstream. Ray crunched across to it, then by judiciously giving line allowed the fish to drift back into the meshes wavering in the flow.

'Prettily done!' I called, as I photographed his net coming up filled with brawny brown trout, quite the equal of mine in condition and practically as big- and stuffed like mine with those small snails drifting so steadily down …

Being in the right place at the right time is vital for memorable trouting, so it is clearly worth noting

'1.7 kg, it was a beautifully-shaped trout in superb condition.'

*Rocky pool on Tasmania's little North Esk River. Productive currents are
obvious, and nearer water is particularly popular with brownies like these ...*

the potential of small sidestreams ... and of drifting
food.

Like humans, trout value a comfortable existence.
They value both shelter from the elements and
protection from those that would do them harm,
clean, stable surroundings and the chance to
reproduce their kind. But to enjoy any of these
things, enough food is basic.

For all creatures, the energy used to obtain food
must at least be matched by the energy derived
from that food and the easier it is to feed, the
better. So far as trout are concerned, this usually
means the heavier the build-up of suitable items of
food, the better.

A key factor in this build-up is drift. Drift
concentrates trout food through major currents or
wind, or both. In streams, major currents are of
obvious importance and for the angler fishing big
water from a bank, places where they collide with it
should be checked carefully. The fly, lure or bait

should come down on or in the current, where a
fish is expecting to see it. Fortunately, it is usually
best placed on the near side of the flow, which is
also nearest to a fish holding in a feeding lie in
slower water between bank and current.

'Feeding lies' are self-explanatory. But trout in
moving water also have 'holding lies' which they
occupy for most of the time when not feeding-and
which for our snail feeders were probably far away.
Such lies are chosen using as criteria the factors
other than food-gathering which follow in later
chapters of this book.

Where a main current flows parallel with and
close to a bank, and especially in a 'flat' river of the
meadows, little bays are popular with trout, as they
are also in thick waterweed such as those fleshy,
tubular 'stick weeds' which are such snares for
hooks. When food is about, current flowing beside
beds of these spike-rushes certainly hold fish,
attracted also by the proximity of cover from

predators which the thick weed provides.

Trout as usual, facing upstream, sometimes lie in a current through the rushes themselves, if they are not too thick. Together with other floating food, mayfly duns may get caught up there or climb the stems, and the spinners to follow may also rest on them next to dragonflies, and particularly some species of damselflies. A place where such currents leave the rushes at the head of a deep, slow pool usually has several trout rising during a hatch, and often some of them are big fish.

In rivers of faster flow, however, holding rocks rather than weeds, tails of pools are favoured by fish because food is thickest there. Also, because the water usually flows more slowly, fish are both more comfortable and have more time to select what food they want without the risk of making a serious mistake. The next best feeding lie is often at the head of the pool where the main current enters, especially if there is quieter water to either side.

Trout will lie in such water but again on the edge of the current, not only because some shelter is nearby in the form of a ruffled water surface but because they are also looking for food there.

Back-eddies where secondary currents peel off the main flow, curl upriver and take some of the food with them will have some fish in residence, probably in the slack water. Eddies in mid river are normally not so big but can also be productive, especially when food collects in them of an evening. So rises are easier to spot, they need to be between the angler and the sun's afterglow. As could be expected, dry flies cast to such eddies will drift afloat and without drag for only short distances, but with pleasing frequency this can be sufficient for trout feeding hard while some light remains.

Places where food items are swept together are very important indeed. These are to be found where currents meet, either converging at slight angles in mid river or where side channels, gutters

'to flounder among the tussocks.'

and tributaries join the main flow. Especially during brief, minor floods, many trout prefer to wait in the main river, not only where back eddies sweep food like worms into places like backwaters but also at their mouths for terrestrial food and those aquatic snails to be swept down, rather than swimming up them.

When mercury climbing into the twenties enlivens trout tucker and water remain high enough for long enough, small sidewaters are obviously worth a look. Yet when levels fall, flow ceases and the 'conveyor belt' stops, trout are also likely to enter deeper sidewaters in search of food. Good spots to try are at the heads of ditches, and in larger sidewaters just above where they rejoin the main stream.

Wind can also be vital in sweeping food together, and on lakes can be the sole agent of drift. Others on lakes include feeder streams and outlet currents such as the productive one in St Clair Lagoon and another at Tooms Lake when water is spilling over its dam. 'Food funnels' can be formed by the wind between the mainland and an island like Bertram's Island, the main island in Little Pine Lagoon. This particular water on the Central Plateau of Tasmania is noted for its heavy summer hatches of mayflies. The south-westerly which blows with unfortunate strength and regularity over its dam and up the length of the lagoon sweeps the mayfly duns along with it. Thanks to mainland and island, shaped to welcome them with open arms, they tend to bunch

together in the strait and in Scotties Bay just beyond-and so do the trout.

Another Central Plateau water very popular with anglers is Arthurs Lake, and here during a northerly Pylon Bay at the mouth of Cowpaddock Bay has a point of land which acts as one side of a funnel to channel the duns hatching from weedbeds to windward. Not far away at Penstock Lagoon, a favoured area during the season is along the Saplings Shore. Here a point of land lies almost parallel to the westerlies which often blow, and push along insects like duns and sometimes, in autumn, jassid leafhoppers, which bunch together in skeins when they reach the point. Wading anglers fishing from its lee out front to the concentrations of insects can enjoy great sport at times. Every stillwater of course has such contours and winds which, combined with items of prey, influence the location of feeding trout. On a tactical level can be added slicks caused by 'structure' such as logs and rocks along the shore onto which the wind is blowing. Trout in them can see food items better, and often assemble where gaps in such structure channel them together.

Through wave action, wind causes discolouration of shallow areas of stillwaters with silty bottoms and if this is severe, because of problems of vision and respiration expanded on in a later chapter, trout will usually avoid them if they can. Practically the whole of a small lagoon can be affected, although Little Pine Lagoon water is often clearer near its feeder river. On a larger lake, the extent of just how loose and shallow the margins are will determine how dirty the water there becomes. Waters vary and sheltered shores are often best at Lake Sorell, especially earlier in the season, while at Arthurs Lake it is also often best to avoid shores onto which a brisk wind is blowing, or was blowing the day before.

On the other hand, along the rocky shores of Great Lake just over the hill the rougher the water becomes, the better. When Great Lake is high enough, midges and caddis fluttering out among its drowned bushes can make the sheltered shores productive. But at the lower levels usual on this big water, strong waves tear loose food items from the bottom and flush out others from among the rocks normally high and dry along the shore. Trout are at times seen in the faces of waves humping before they break, and less frequently wriggling among the rocks back down to the lake, half in and half out of the water, after being deposited by a retreating wave in their eagerness to feed.

The windward shore is also the place for trout to be when insects like midges, beetles and especially mayfly duns floating on the water are blown there. Anglers will find casting into or at least across that wind an irritation more than compensated for by increased sport. However, after the duns have hatched into the shiny, clear-winged spinners which hover over the shallows to mate and lay eggs, a wind from shore will force some of them down where trout can get at them-especially when high

water levels have brought closer to the shoreline both fishable water and spinners. So if the wind direction has not changed, the angler is well advised to visit the shores opposite, usually after the hatch of duns has ended. An exception would be if you were fishing earlier to duns blowing along the strait between the mainland and an island substantial enough to host good numbers of spinners in its lee, and Scotties Bay in Little Pine Lagoon again comes to mind.

Patches of unruffled, 'oily' water will be found of course along lee shores but will also form into long slicks across the surface of stillwaters, 'wind lanes' where much food can accumulate. These wind lanes seem to be caused in the first place by land contours which channel wind across the surface of the water in fixed directions. Wind distributes surface heat downward in oceans as well as lakes via counter-rotating cylinders of spiralling water currents called 'Langmuir cells', each spinning along a horizontal axis parallel with the surface and the direction of a sustained wind. This downwelling was found in one American lake to extend 10 to 15 metres below the surface and can be quite rapid. Vertical velocity correlates with wind speed and was measured in one large lake at more than 9 cm per second. Surface streaks mark the downwelling which causes not only items of food but also oily material to converge and accumulate, accounting for the name 'surface slicks'. These move downwind faster than the upwelling water adjacent.

If such a wind lane remains in place long enough,

'Ray contorted himself.'

A brownie to remember.

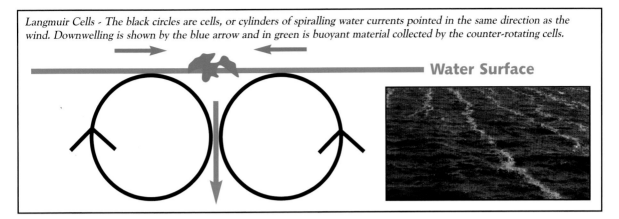

Langmuir Cells - The black circles are cells, or cylinders of spiralling water currents pointed in the same direction as the wind. Downwelling is shown by the blue arrow and in green is buoyant material collected by the counter-rotating cells.

Water Surface

enough food often collects to attract trout in numbers. Chironomid pupae and adults in particular are sought in slicks by trout in Tasmania's highland lakes and while a boat is needed to enjoy fully the sport from lake fish feeding hard on these 'midges' in the wind lanes, wading anglers can intercept many of them on smaller, shallower waters such as those to the west of Great Lake. The place where a wind lane ends, against a dam or the shore, is often worth a look, especially early in the day and to a lesser extent in the evenings.

While various writers have covered slicks in depth-or perhaps, at length-and how they affect trout locations in lakes, the importance of slicks on moving water has received less attention. Working together, the influence of wind and water currents can be significant. Combined with a strong current bearing food on its surface, smooth water in the lee

of higher banks can attract trout because they can see it more easily, a factor to be expanded later in this book. Incidentally, in these circumstances wind can also be used to drift into place on flat water a dry fly placed artfully upwind rather than cast directly to a wary fish.

If the flow is not strong enough to hold floating food in place, the wind may blow it towards the other bank. All is not lost if that bank is substantial and high enough to force the wind upward, allowing a pocket of calm air to form with associated smooth water along its length. Also, flies like mayfly duns and spent spinners will be blown from the grip of the current onto flat water in places like bays and small backwaters, especially when water levels are high. When enough collect, dark triangles which are the noses of large trout often appear among them.

Popular with trout are little bays among rushes, like the one in centre frame where a hefty brown took a prospecting dun in spite of an evil south-easterly and that clouded water coming over Brumbys Creek's Top Weir.

Chapter 2

Trout Food - The Flies

Pleasant sights like substantial nebs will be seen with gratifying frequency if anglers match where they go looking for trout with the sort of food the fish are eating at the time.

Continuing with mayflies, those insects so important to anglers for consistent and predictable sport, much depends on the stage of the hatch. Trout are attracted to nymphs moving about restlessly near the bottom just before rising to the surface to moult into duns. Finding fish feeding efficiently through selection of the one type of prey and gathering it with the same sort of action boils down to finding where the duns are hatching. Tasmanian nymphs like a soft bottom and weeds for shelter and seem to hatch first in the shallows where the water is warmer. Much depends, however, on local knowledge, on knowing for example that if the water level of Arthurs Lake fell to low last year, this summer it may be best to look for nymphing fish over last year's shallows and weedbeds which are now well out from shore.

The next stage of the mayfly hatch is marked by the appearance of duns on the surface and at this time on stillwater a quick tour in a boat is useful to find where they are thickest. On streams there is no substitute for walking and looking. Noting day by day where duns appear gives the observant angler an idea of where to find, upwind or upcurrent, active nymphs when fishing early the next day.

Anglers without a boat will be helped in finding concentrations of duns on stillwater by the busyness of birds like ravens stumping about importantly and picking at them along the margins, and occasionally by ducks and even seagulls in the shallows. The clumping together of boats may also help, though quite often this is caused by a 'snowball' effect rather than the actual presence of duns. When the hatch is tailing off or has just ended, patches of thick weed on the surface often act as reservoirs, trapping duns or perhaps giving them a resting place during the hatch. When it is finished, steady trickles of duns continue to drift off downwind of them, usually to the interest of cruising trout and of those which seem to sometimes take up temporary residence among the weeds.

At times in a heavy hatch, feeding trout can be seen everywhere. But those most likely to take one particular dun are often those looking about in confined spaces, places with obvious boundaries such as-and especially-patches of open water among weedbeds which reach to the surface.

The final mayfly stage is the spinner, of particular attraction to trout in moving water and bringing to mind my outing on a major flat river in northern Tasmania one recent spring.

Good trout were leaping and slashing at the large, delicate flies flickering over the water, so I wasted no time in jointing my rod and fluffing out the hackles of the Red Spinner already attached. I turned back a peckish tiddler a few minutes later and, when a nice brownie came to net soon afterwards, rubbed my hands in anticipation of an afternoon filled with red letter sport.

Nearly every spring this particular bend, and the mouth of the short but deep and weedy little backwater immediately below it, were hotspots for dry fly sport from moving fish, but right now I decided to rest the water and moved on upstream. Past experience left me a trifle peeved but unsurprised at the marked fall in fishy activity just a few hundred metres away.

I did manage several reasonable brownies which

Atalophlebia australis dun.

Typical medium black spinner habitat.

were sipping and jumping now and then at flickering black flies not quite as big-but walked quite a distance to find them, and then had to bide my time in the bushes while trying to get into step with the irregular rhythms of their rising.

Back at the bend late that afternoon and a good deal less toey, I was both gratified and just slightly irritated to find the fish again going hard at the same big flies, some black, most of them red.

But why only here? I'd concluded some seasons before that one reason must be the wall of willows on the other, northern bank which broke the force of the prevailing winds so well-as did the sheer earthen bank on the other side of the flowless little backwater. But was there another reason?

Perhaps it was the thought of the lack of flow in that same short length which prompted me to recall the other expanse of still water close by-at the upper end of the bend, where quite a large, rushy, permanent pond out in the paddock was linked to the river itself by a gutter, narrow but deep enough to be difficult to wade across even in summer.

Might the thickness of these big red and black spinners, of such interest to the trout, have anything to do with the amount of still water in this particular area? Research was needed...

Mayflies occur throughout Australia-most abundantly in Tasmania and the highlands of south eastern Australia. Numerous species also exist in the colder parts of east coast streams as far north as Cape York Peninsula, a few species are found in the slow inland streams in eastern states and several others appear in the south west of WA.

All mayfly nymphs need relatively unpolluted water, both running and still. None can tolerate any trace of saltiness. Nymphs of each species are normally restricted to a particular type of habitat, ranging from stones in high, cold, snow-melt streams to the stagnant lowland backwaters favoured by only a few species which, however, include some vitally important for angling sport.

For trout anglers in southern Australia, probably the most important mayflies are contained within the widespread genus *Atalophlebia*. This is the largest genus of the Leptophlebiidae, the dominant family making up fully 70% of all the Australian species of mayflies.

Atalophlebia mayflies include such well-known

Black Spinner after emergence from dun shuck. Photo: Mick Hall

trout insects as red spinners, large black spinners and penstock browns.

The nymphs of these three mayflies all prefer slow or still water. The nymph of the red spinner *Atalophlebia australis* is a sluggish crawler found in slow or still water clinging under cover such as stones and logs. While the large black spinner *A. albiterminata* is widespread throughout both highland and lowland Tasmania, like the red spinner it is most numerous on slower-flowing rivers and its nymph finds slower pools and slack water in lagoons and backwaters to its liking. This nymph, which can live in stagnant water, is found in thick water-weed and sometimes partly buried under stones and logs.

By definition, mayflies common in lakes favour still water. The species now arguably most numerous in total numbers up on Tasmania's Central Plateau is *Atalophlebia superba*, the penstock brown whose nymph is quite a rapid swimmer found on the bottom among thick weed and detritus.

The other major mayfly of the Plateau is the highland spinner, *Tasmanophlebia ancestries*, whose nymph is active and free-swimming and also prefers still or slow water where it settles into sand or silt. On the mainland of Australia, related mayfly species range from the Barrington Tops in southern NSW to South Australia's Fleurieu Peninsula just south of Adelaide. Their nymphs prefer upland lakes, and the slow-flowing reaches of usually small streams.

Other mayflies commonly met with on trout waters include the small black spinner *Nousia deliculata*, which prefers streams of slow to moderate flow at lower altitudes. The nymph is found in the shallows below stones and logs-and its inconspicuous little adult is more important than would at first appear.

As well as appearing over a wider variety of streams, the small black spinner has the pleasant habits of tolerating dull or windy weather better than other local mayflies and, by hovering in swarms over the one spot, encourages trout to feed more predictably on it.

Sized in between the large and small black spinners is the medium black, whose nymph is a very active runner which clings to the bottom of

Typical brown nymph. Photo: Mick Hall

Red spinner

stones and prefers highland or lowland streams-in this case, of moderate to fast flow.

While such mayflies of faster water as the medium black spinner certainly stimulate wonderful angling sport along many of the 'streamy' stretches of our trout streams, it's plain that the nymphs of Australia's main species of mayflies prefer the water of lakes and slower streams-probably not surprisingly, in light of how much more common such water is in the driest of continents.

Feeding ceases during a nymph's final instars, or stages of growth, and it often moves to another habitat during this period. But such a move is usually not far, frequently being merely towards the side of the stream where it will eventually emerge. Since the adult usually doesn't move far either, finding memorable angling sport sparked by important mayflies such as large red spinners and black spinners large and small really hinges on...finding where their preferred habitat is most extensive.

Since this habitat is in still or slow water, finding where such mayflies will be thickest seems

to me to boil down to finding such water. Sometimes this is in the stream's main channel itself, in larger bays and corners and over shallow, weedy shelves. More often it is in places off to the side such as backwaters, billabongs, marshes, sidewaters, lagoons, ponds, smaller basins, saucers and other depressions.

I've long appreciated the importance of such habitat on a 'strategic' level, and therefore in October would never be far away from a place like the Stewarton property on Tasmania's Macquarie River if I could help it. The red spinners hatching in such numbers along this particular stretch of that storied flat trout-stream of the meadows, largely from the extensive marshes and sidewaters nearby, attract most flyfishers far more powerfully to Stewarton than to the narrower, more streamy stretches of the very same river only a kilometre or so away which host relatively few mayflies-understandably, medium black spinners.

This knowledge can be used tactically to choose specific spots within the same stretch of other rivers, perhaps on the one property.

Compatible for the mayflies of particular

interest may well be the entire lengths of a few streams such as the Break O'Day River, that flat, slow little eastern Tasmanian tributary of the South Esk, but habitats vary from one stretch to another along the main river, and along most others. On an unfamiliar trout stream, how then can suitably flowless water be located?

Inspection from the air is an option. Cheaper are the detailed aerial photographs available in Tasmania from Tasmap and including the well-known Stewarton, which clearly shows the actual features of interest to an angler. Cheaper yet are 1: 100 000 maps such as 'South Esk' which also includes the Stewarton stretch-and which by also showing 'land subject to inundation', can indicate general areas worth closer inspection. After that, precise information on the location of features such as minor watercourses, swamps and standing water down to pond size is shown in the 1:25 000 series, in sufficient detail to allow anglers to get down to the nitty-gritty of pinpointing just where to try.

When actually fishing the water chosen, pools and runs with strong currents are best, holding the flies on the water longer. Deep, narrow runs, just below places where duns are hatching, bunch them together and may be worth prospecting early in the hatch. On slower water, duns tend to flutter ashore shortly after hatching. In times of a big flood, food will be scattered everywhere, but during a moderate flood, with the stream just over its higher banks, the flow over the main channel is usually best if it can be reached with safety.

The final stage of the mayfly hatch is normally the most spectacular and productive on streams, with trout leaping and slashing at the spinners in the air when they first appear in numbers. If there is no wind, spinners are to be found all along the margins and while mating clouds of some species like small black spinners tend to hover in the one place, other species move without pattern across and beside the water.

If the wind does begin to blow, some species of mayflies overseas continue to fly but local spinners seek shelter in streamside vegetation or, if the breeze is not too strong, remain airborne in the lee of thick clumps of it. Pools sheltered by willows or protected by high tussocks or sheer banks will often repay a visit at this time, especially if deep water lies close to shelter, on waters as diverse as lowland rivers and highland tarns.

When the females start laying eggs, most doing so by repeatedly dipping the tips of their abdomens into the water as they slowly fly over it, on rivers they counter the effects of the flow on the dispersal of eggs by flying upstream and find stretches of faster water especially attractive. These stretches may be the best places to look for spinners, especially when the hatch is thin, waxing or waning.

Look for shelter from wind-and deeper, narrow runs that bunch duns together.

Their main mission in life accomplished, the spinners fall spent to the surface of the river, sometimes on the currents where concentrations attracting trout certainly include tiny caenid spinners early on calm summer mornings, and sometimes on slack water, where after a heavy hatch they may be found in rafts. On many days these are the places to visit, to fish for trout quietly and methodically mopping up the remains.

On stillwaters, places with defined boundaries, such as holes in weedbeds, may have trout lying on station waiting for duns and spinners to drift over them. These fish are much more predictable than those cruising and feeding in more open water, especially when a warm breeze is encouraging the duns to get airborne quickly. Trout may also gather in oily slicks, where they can better see food in or on the water. Since

at Brumbys Creek. Large green stoneflies are rarely taken, perhaps because of an unpleasant taste which would act as a defence mechanism.

Following mayflies, caddis are probably the insects next in fly fishing importance. Their nymphs in the shape of stick caddis are common in practically all waters from highland lakes to lowland streams, especially in riffles. Adult caddis, like spinners but in the evenings rather

feeding, while less exciting, is now so much easier than it was at the beginning of the hatch, and bearing in mind the energy equation about input at least equalling output, many of the fish now feeding so earnestly are big ones.

Stoneflies such as the small brown *Leptoperla* fluttering over the water can be mistaken for early duns but are taken by trout only occasionally, and practically never on waters such as the Top Weir

than in the full light of day, favour a surface protected by wind and with deeper water nearby. On rivers, various trees can at times host localised clouds of caddis fluttering around them.

The rivers of the meadows, many of them middle-aged and slower in flow, may in places have isolated willow trees which, on occasional afternoons and evenings from late in spring until the middle of autumn, are surrounded thickly

*Typical small snowflak
caddis (shown here greatl
enlarged), found aroun
willows and tea tree o
many Australian streams
Photo: Mick Ha*

enough by caddis to attract trout. On headwaters or on more youthful streams of thinner, but more boisterous and noisier broken flow, caddis like to roost on tea trees. So among the very best places for prospecting dry flies are brisk, deeper runs underneath or just downstream from such trees growing over them.

In Tasmania, tea trees along the shore over deeper water may also attract trout to caddis fluttering around them on stillwaters which lie at hill height, such as Lake Sorell. Above 1 000 metres, on waters like many of the western lakes on the Central Plateau, their place is taken by pencil pines. In the highlands in summer, evening darkness becomes complete.

Also in summer evenings on stillwaters, nymphs of the insect order Odonata may interest trout as they swim to shore. In particular, dragonfly nymphs, or 'mudeyes' as they are more commonly known, use jets of water from their rears to propel themselves jerkily to dry land. They emerge and climb onto structures such as rocks and bushes to metamorphose into the adult form, which is also of considerable interest to fish.

Naturally enough, anglers need to seek out waters with large numbers of dragonflies. Evening sport is sometimes available in season on the weirs of Brumbys Creek, near Cressy. I remember

One Brumbys Creek trout feeding among the rushes had eaten at least 75 blue damselflies.

rises to caddis are quite good on some waters and poor on others. Visitors will benefit from the local knowledge given freely on request by host anglers, Fisheries rangers and those behind the counters of tackle shops.

Usually to be preferred is the lee shore, particularly where any wind first meets the water. Although this is the best place to be, with luck the chosen spot will lie between the angler and the afterglow later in the evening which makes it much easier to spot fish feeding, not only in river eddies but also in these highland lakes where they will often only take the floating fly just before

being beaten on the Top Weir one dull evening early in December by large trout which were surging along and sometimes through the surface in their eagerness to feed. They ignored my mayfly dun and twitched nymph comprehensively but I managed to take some next day from the same place. A post-mortem revealed many mudeyes.

Other waters which can usually be depended on for productive mudeye fishing are waters formed relatively recently: Lake Burbury, a hydro lake in western Tasmania which first filled in 1992, and in northern Tasmania Four Springs Lake near

The river backwater with bend behind, referred to on page 10.

Westbury which was opened to angling in 1999. In this instance there again is no substitute for local knowledge.

It is often a real challenge to interest trout leaping at adult damselflies and dragonflies, especially on the Brumbys Creek weirs where fish not only have been thoroughly 'educated' through fishing pressure but have rich pickings readily available down among the weeds if things get too hectic at the surface. Best sport often involves anglers finding trout feeding in limited areas. This they tend to do anyway when the big flies first appear, but later random cruising poses major problems for predicting where lures should be placed. Trout may patrol smaller areas such as slicks in the lee of shelter if wind ruffles the surface severely enough to restrict their vision in open water. For the same reason, they may remain in the one area as daylight fades. Physical barriers such as beds of thick rushes may also help the angler's cause. A light ripple is best for fussy fish, and at Brumbys this means a southerly or easterly wind to balance the daily north westerly sea breeze which is boosted by the same heat that enlivens Odonata.

Sport to Odonata is more consistent on rivers, especially from trout holding in currents through their pools and runs and needing to make menu choices quickly, and on the smaller, more barren streams where the menu of the trout is much more restricted in variety and quantity. So far as dry flies are concerned, splashers to Odonata are usually nowhere near as discriminating as they are on larger, more fertile waters and, if presented properly, various floaters such as dun, beetle and grasshopper ties will be accepted with pleasing frequency.

As mentioned in the first chapter, pockets among the rushes are worth checking at times, particularly when damselflies are hovering over them and resting on the plants. I have seen on several occasions along the Macquarie River the spectacular sight of trout going after damselflies by flying horizontally through the rushes with jaws agape.

Chironomids or 'midges' are taken freely by trout from late in spring, through summer and into autumn. Since midge nymphs prefer still or slow water, they are particularly important in lakes. Wind lanes have been mentioned in the

Lagoon, for example, midges hatch freely from among the pin-rushes growing on the banks of the river which winds through it, banks which are submerged at the height now maintained on this lagoon during summer.

When lake levels rise and drown bushes, and remain high for several years as Tasmania's Great Lake did in the mid 1990s, dry fly fishing can be good especially with an off-shore breeze. Midges breed in the rotting bushes and venture especially in summer onto the water early and late in the day.

Along with midges, another member of the two-winged order of insects known as Diptera, and in adult form rather similar to the mosquito, is the sub-family *Chaoborus*. This fly is transparent in its larval zooplankton or 'wriggler' stage, is known as a 'phantom midge' and shelters in the depths or in sediments during the day. At night, however, phantom midges migrate to the surface and sometimes cover 15 vertical metres in large lakes. Weak swimmers, they prefer stillwaters but remain at the mercy of currents and are often drawn into wind lanes where small fish feeding on them may in turn attract trout. Obviously the best time to fish wind lanes is at night, or for sight-fishers at first or last light.

In moving water, only rivers with significant stretches of slow flow have midges hatching in sufficient numbers to interest some trout. Suitable stretches are where the water slows and spreads out in bulges and broadwaters. If it is also shallow, so much the better, as explained in the chapter on trout senses.

previous chapter and since insects in general find it difficult to colonise the depths of freshwater lakes, also relevant in predicting where midging trout will be found is the location of the shallower areas where hatches are frequently heaviest. As well as along margins and in bays, shallows of importance can be on the tops of islands and river banks just below the surface. In Little Pine

mselfly

Chapter 3

Trout Food - Terrestrials

Beetles as well as flies can be relied on to interest trout. Given their immense variety and the pleasant habit some have of appearing in large numbers over a short period of time, beetles inspire occasional spells of intense feeding, together with less hectic but usually more consistent action during much of the season. An imitation of a small black beetle floating on top or fished underneath at various depths, either motionless or twitched, is arguably Tasmania's most effective single trout lure over a full season.

The searching wet beetle is frequently effective

Rising water filling this river backwater should soon be followed by trout.

in spring on streams, especially in the shallower areas of the deeper, slower rivers of the meadows. During many autumns on these rivers, black beetles come down with some regularity in the surface film, on occasion together with ants and less often with those little spiders which get airborne on silken threads. All these creatures are accepted avidly by trout keen to build up condition for spawning, and winter. Finding trout which are feeding on them, and are catchable, involves choosing a river of good flow rather than one where water is so low, slow and clear that fish flee in panic before any cast is completed. If autumn rainfall has been scanty, anglers may need to choose 'tailwater' fisheries, rivers receiving water from hydroelectric generation, which in Tasmania include Brumbys Creek and the lower stretches of the Macquarie River linked with it. Water in a few other rivers like the Elizabeth and

Lake may also be raised artificially by releases of water from storage dams and lakes for irrigation and domestic use.

Once a suitable 'flat' river has been chosen, tactics on it are simple: walk upstream, and look for rises. These will often be in midstream where various currents meet and sweep food together. Precise casting is needed, and a rod with sufficient backbone to put a fly like a small Red Tag, Peacock and Black or similar pattern well out on the water.

More complicated are the preparations needed to fish effectively the occasional heavy fall at last light of the cockchafer beetles *Adoryphorus couloni* on flat rivers early in spring. Most important is choosing a suitable place, and the key factor in this is drift, in this case the result of major currents marshalling these chunky, black beetles so that they come down frequently enough to persuade trout within casting range that it is worth their while to rise to them. Also important in persuading fish is the ease with which they can track their prey, so a smooth water surface is essential. If there is wind, the spot chosen should be sheltered from it, perhaps by willows. Vital also is the adequacy of the angler's own vision in seeing rises in the gloom, so that, as with eddies and evening caddis, trout should rise between the angler and the afterglow of sunset. Finally, as darkness falls, casting should not be restricted by obstacles like gorse bushes and hawthorn trees.

Obviously, such a place may take some finding but one consolation is that it, or stretches nearby, will often suit fish slashing at the end of summer and early in autumn at the large corbie moths *Oncopera intricata*, which also come out in force at last light as indeed do most other moths, nocturnal in habits to avoid their main predators- birds. The appearance of *O. intricata* may be preceded by the swarming in December of the reddish-brown 'winter corbie' *Oncopera rufobrunnae*, found throughout south-eastern Australia but in Tasmania limited to the north.

Cockchafer beetle

Trout in a pool fed by a single current are often more willing to take grasshoppers.

These moths differ from the bogong moths of the mainland which fly to highlands such as the Australian Alps in summer, although one or two bogongs may occasionally be found in north eastern Tasmania after being blown across Bass Strait.

Drift is less important for corbie moths because such large insects, which swarm on some warm, calm evenings to mate on the ground, cause a commotion anywhere on the water as soon as they blunder onto it. Open banks allow the angler to move freely and smartly enough to present a large floater without delay to cruising trout. If these banks are covered with rank grass so much the better, because female moths seek out such growth to lay their eggs in to protect them.

Corbie Moth

During the days of summer and on through autumn, grasshoppers finding themselves on the water are nutritious additions to the trout's bill of fare, which shrinks somewhat as other insects seek shelter from the hot sun. Heat serves only to liven up grasshoppers, and a carefree leap from a steep bank on a lazy summer day may well result in disaster, especially for grasshoppers which cannot fly back to safety.

Important to trout is the wingless grasshopper found throughout southern Australia and in New Zealand, *Phaulacridium vittatum*.

Grasshoppers are particularly important insects for anglers on moving water, attracted as they are to the thicker growth along river banks. During many summers they are common enough to be a major food item in southern states of Australia, although in Tasmania they usually occur along the rivers only in localised concentrations. Nevertheless, they are widespread enough to interest the little trout of the fast waters in the foothills as well as the fish of the farmlands with which they are more usually associated.

Wingless grasshoppers may well be particularly numerous along stretches of river where a dry spring or overstocking by farmers have thinned out the dense grass which bars many young insects from the clovers and flatweeds upon which they feed. In choosing water to fish, anglers should bear these factors in mind, as well as looking for crops being harvested near rivers, all of which encourage adult grasshoppers to move to the more luxuriant vegetation on the banks of rivers, from where they are more likely to land on the water.

How well any particular stretch of river bank suits grasshoppers can soon be tested by a walk along it; but even if they are plentiful everywhere, certain parts will be better for sport than others. Most fish interested in grasshoppers naturally lie not in midstream but next to, or just downstream from, the banks where hoppers are more likely to be found, especially where banks border deeper water and a steady current strong enough to hold them in its grip. The angler should pay close attention to any such bank which is also high, sheer and topped with grass, in particular if its base is indented with little bays where trout can hold in slower water while monitoring the current for grasshoppers floating past on or in it.

Where the river is not large, the angler will often find that trout in pools fed by a single current rather than several will be more willing to take a grasshopper. As well as near banks, on larger rivers productive stretches for wading are wide, rippled, weedy runs, as are the edges of major currents flowing three or four metres out from the bank. On any river, trout as usual are more likely to be watching moving water rather than slack, and even if it is next to the bank, shallow, clear water is usually hopeless-especially when the sun is shining.

In finding trout feeding on other terrestrials, the location of vegetation which may host

Wingless grasshopper Phaulacridium vittatum

Yellow-bellied or 'trouserbrace' hopper, genus Praxibulus

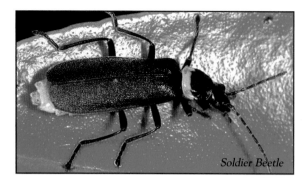
Soldier Beetle

them needs to be considered. The long-horned grasshoppers of the Tettigoniidae family, slender, elongated and frequently green, feed and live on the foliage of various native trees and just sometimes find themselves on the water below them. Host vegetation like the buzzy burr also plays a similar role in locating fish feeding on army caterpillars, minor because these creatures go on the march through crops so rarely. More important, however, are willows as hosts for the tiny green aphids which appear in myriads on their new leaves. When enough drop to the water, these may well provide the fisher of the floating fly with the first sport of the season in the full light of day. Streams associated with aphids are the smaller, deeper ones with stretches walled by willows, such as Tasmania's North Esk and Liffey Rivers.

The role in hosting caddis of both isolated willows along the larger rivers of the meadows and of clumps of tea trees along the streams of broken flow has been mentioned in the previous chapter. Tea trees also host the black and brown beetles known unsurprisingly as tea tree beetles, which can occur in summer in numbers where patches of these trees border rivers like the St Patricks, Meander, Lake and lower South Esk, and stillwaters like Lake Sorell. Although concentrations of these beetles are localised in time and place, anglers will eventually find it to their advantage to check the foliage of tea trees occasionally for them and to carry a few floating imitations. One specialised tie created by Dick Wigram has a body of black ostrich herl, black cock hackle and a brown wing case of hen's wing quill.

Also useful will be copies of another beetle, the green and yellow soldier beetle of the Cantharidae family which is sometimes widespread in summer, mainly in the lowlands and often found with tea tree beetles. Noel Jetson has developed a small dry fly with a body of yellow wool, a black head

Alvin Cooke about to net a hefty South Esk River trout which took his grasshopper. Note the magnificent bank for them to hop from, just upstream.

and several turns of black cock hackle. Wing covers are of green quill, tied in flat and in a slight 'vee' shape.

These beetles can spark early-summer sport worth remembering.

One recent Christmas, northern Tasmania's South Esk River ran low, and clear....but briskly enough to have a few trout on the fin, I would have thought.

Yet no fish moved early that afternoon except a few oncers, slashing every now and then presumably at scattered damselflies or dragonflies. I wasn't surprised, because no flies were showing on the stream's surface, nor could I spot any fish in the gravelly shallows except for a couple of tiddlers that fled in panic at my distant approach.

Sticky in body waders, I began to feel dispirited in the strong sunshine. A doe, probably an escapee from one of the herds of deer farmed elsewhere in the area, appeared at the edge of the next pool above. Although not looking my way, its stance and restless ears suggested unease; I wasn't surprised when it vanished like smoke.

Eventually I approached the foot of one of the best pools. It was sheltered and partly shaded by a few flanking willows and a windmill along one bank, and half a dozen tea tree bushes along the other. These bushes grew densely, were forced well out over the water by a thick, high wall of gorse behind-and the white flowers on some were probably covered with more of the beetles I'd

noticed on several other, isolated tea tree bushes nearby.

Rarely did no fish show in this pool in warmer weather, due in part perhaps to the food and shelter furnished to trout from thick weed growing on a bed abruptly deeper-at least waist deep in fact, and I had to watch my step for holes just here. The river was narrower too, so the water still flowed briskly, and in several distinct paths.

As I watched, a couple of trout showed in these currents up near the tea trees and another, closer fish twice rose well. To beetles? I wondered, lengthening line to cover it as soon as possible with my size 12 Brown Dun. Under went the fly in fine style, I struck fast as usual and out flew a short, deep-bodied trout of around a kilogram which finished its dive among a clump of weed. These jumpers so often do, I thought as I waded up to it, and this one has probably been hooked before...perhaps by me.

Taking the leader cautiously in hand, I could feel the trout still attached. Out it rushed, across current and into even shallower weed where its broad flank could be seen gleaming silver in the sun. Counting it caught, I waded across leisurely, the fish burrowed deeper into the weed, which I parted while pulling at the leader again...but all that came out this time was a drowned and slimy Brown Dun.

Nothing now showed just above either, and prospecting the currents

The Brown Dun is a good all-rounder on the South Esk River.

again proved useless.

On upstream I trudged, pausing atop a high bank to admire two large trout that I could see quite clearly with the naked eye, lying motionless in full sun near the mouth of 'The Breakaway', a broad side-channel that flowed down through the paddocks during floods.

Today it was short, scarcely knee-deep, and crystal clear. But damselflies were hovering in force over fringing weed here, and a heavy splash confirmed why these fish were prepared to expose themselves so casually. Yet besotted with damselflies they assuredly were not; although I stood motionless, they seemed like the deer to become aware of my gaze-and vanished just as unobtrusively.

Mid-afternoon and too bright, too low and clear, I thought-but it had been heartening to see a few trout looking to feed with some purpose at

last, and they were decent ones, too. I rounded a bend and peered over another sheer bank to spy one more big fish, literally under my feet, on the lookout just below the surface of a bankside gutter among thick strapweed that swayed gently in the current. Although I stood stock-still again, it too wasted no time in ghosting away downstream.

Making a mental note to look for it on my way back, I pressed on upriver hoping to find tea tree bushes, because I was now sure that the fish I'd missed had been taking the small, elongated tea tree beetles so attracted to their white flowers that in some summers they would swarm on them like bees.

Onward I tramped as the rays of the sun began to lengthen, vexed to find few tea trees. Willows were everywhere as usual, along with other exotics and when I eventually did come up to a small clump of tea trees, they weren't properly in flower and no beetles or trout showed near them. Another single bush that leaned out over the river some distance ahead, however, glowed white in parts and I trudged to it.

The sight of a long, grey shape suspended in the shade below the outer edge of this tea tree revived my interest. Fortunately, a wide, shallow shelf enabled me to wade into position for a clear cast and I flicked the Brown Dun towards the overhanging bush. It landed just short, and floated down unheeded.

Hadn't the fish spotted it ... or was it the wrong fly? If I'd seen fish feeding persistently, or had been ignored by that first and only fish hooked, I may have tied on a more exact, size 14 imitation: perhaps Dick Wigram's old black and brown tie or Noel Jetson's yellow and green.

I stayed with my Brown Dun, as good a fly to prospect the South Esk as any I knew, once the first of the season's mayflies had appeared on it. The next cast again dropped short, and a little farther out, but the trout must have seen it land and I marvelled at the silvery-grey shape angling upward through the clear water. It took well and came to net after a short, sharp tussle-a rather slim but shapely brownie a little short of a kilogram.

In its stomach were both kinds of tea tree beetles, especially the black and brown ones, and

Early autumn evening on the lower Macquarie and a slash at a corbie moth.

The white flowers on tea trees sometimes attract swarms of tea tree and soldier beetles early in summer.

little else. Feeling just as happy about this as about landing the fish itself, and with my watch showing 6.00 p.m., I set off back downstream direct to the bend, and the bank...and yes, there was the trout, lying in the same gutter but deeper in the water this time.

Out went the same Brown Dun, with me giving it enough slack to counter the upsetting twitch upon landing that can happen when casting from a height. Over the fish it floated...nothing. I cast again, this time the Dun fell just a little more forcibly-and obviously within the trout's window, because it plainly went to action stations and slanted upwards without delay.

A firm take, the usual instant strike and away went the fish-downstream again, but furiously this time. It streaked under a thick patch of strapweed waving on the surface and into clear water beyond, then with the line held down by the weed, rocketed upward among an explosion of silver shrapnel-and I had to bid that good old Brown Dun adieu.

With the sun sinking, my outing ended at The Breakaway, where a heavy splash announced that good trout were after those damselflies again. An evening breeze had sprung up, and I used it to drift a Red Spinner downwind over several fish. One half-rose in the ripple, probably more curious than keen-and if it did so with mixed emotions, I thought I knew how it was feeling ...

I'd done much walking and much looking for little angling action-but what else could you expect, on such a bright summer day with few flies about?

Yet I felt pleased that observation and a little thought had enabled me to make the most of limited opportunities involving some of the South Esk's larger fish, and reflected on the importance in the trout's scheme of things of beetles-and of vegetation. It provides shelter and shade, and hosts valuable items of food above and below water.

As well as tea trees, some silver wattles all over the state may also carry beetles, in this case

Pyroides orphana, a Chrysomelid gum beetle of the Paropsine group. This insect is commonly known as the fireblight beetle, because of the scorched appearance of the host silver wattles following its feeding on their foliage in winter and spring. Adults are small and dome-shaped, greenish with cream and brown stripes along their wing covers and are most common in early summer and autumn along lowland rivers.

Much more likely to be encountered, feeding in this instance on the leaves of gums rather than wattles, and especially in the highlands in summer and to a lesser extent in autumn, is another Chrysomelid gum beetle, the Tasmanian eucalyptus leaf beetle *Chrysophtharta bimaculata*, which arguably is the most notorious insect pest of the state's forests. *C. bimaculata* adults are like ladybird beetles in being rounded and dome-shaped. They are often pale pearly green with two distinct black marks near their heads. These beetles have red colour phases and other gum beetles are coloured pale pink, yellow, black, brown and grey, but usually, as for the fireblight beetle, an imitation with an overall green appearance will suffice, fished either dry to moving fish or deep in the water to represent the drowned insect.

Since various gum beetles have been found on the full range of Tasmanian eucalypts, they can be expected throughout the state. Anglers on the Central Plateau, however, are most likely to encounter them and with *C. bimaculata* being the species most common there, knowledge of which specific gums it favours is obviously necessary for deciding where it may be thickest. These are *Eucalyptus regnans*, swamp or stringybark, and two other species closely related to it: *E. delegatensis* and *E. obliqua*, which are stringybarks. Also attacked is *E. vernicosa*, the little varnished gum of the western highlands.

When numerous, gum beetles will be found on some days sprinkling the surface of many highland stillwaters. From personal experience, these will certainly include Lake Sorell and Arthurs Lake, Dee and Little Pine Lagoons and the Great Lake, where the well-known Great Lake Beetle floater may well imitate a species or colour phase of a gum beetle. On this lake I have enjoyed good sport on warm days casting a dry fly from a rocky bluff into a fresh breeze which, thanks to the drift mentioned in the first chapter, has arranged a smorgasbord at its foot, with gum

beetles as the main course for large trout which ghost up at times from the depths. On the other hand, fish may cruise at night into the shallows of stillwaters such as Arthurs Lake to feast on rafts of gum beetles caught in shoreline weed.

A good deal more down to earth are the trout of lowland streams during the times of flood which usually happen early in the season. Although drowned slugs may be of limited and localised interest when a river breaks its banks, much more important are worms flushed out by the rising tide.

In choosing stretches to fish, anglers could with advantage check the ground beside likely-looking water for worms under logs, rocks and cow pats. If none is found, and they may well be scarce if the winter just there has been a dry one, further exploration is indicated. Where worms are plentiful, because of the trout's sense of smell the next step is to choose water with no flow through it as outlined in the later chapter on trout senses. Also mentioned there is the importance of water depth and the stretch chosen should certainly cover ground where trout can see worms with ease. Heavy plant cover is obviously to be avoided and so is an expanse of completely barren ground. To be preferred is a bottom with patches clear of growth or of sparse, short stubble. One small depression on the edge of a paddock of stubble into which the South Esk occasionally spills in spring comes clearly to mind.

Tea Tree Beetle

Litoria raniformis (Green and golden frog)

Chapter 4

Trout Food - Frogs, Snails, Scud

Knowing the natural histories of creatures which fall accidentally onto the water and of others which spend part of their lives in it is important to anglers, but so too is knowing about creatures like snails, scud and other fish which share it with trout for a lifetime. Since water is very important to amphibians, frogs can be included as well.

From the angler's viewpoint, not as much has been written about frogs as perhaps they deserve, so more detail on them and on their importance to trout seems warranted. Fortunately, thanks to scientists such as A.A. Martin and M.J. Littlejohn and books like their *Tasmanian Amphibians,* flowing through to accessible sources such as the Tasmanian Government website at www.tas.gov.au, much new information is now available.

There are several hundred species of frogs in Australia, and of the eleven species in Tasmania three are restricted to the state. One of these eleven, the green and golden bellfrog *Litoria raniformis,* was reported in 1994 to be in decline throughout Australia and was classified as 'vulnerable' in Tasmania. The future of the striped marsh frog is also of concern but most of the state's other nine species were found to be in ample numbers and widespread.

Susceptible to changes in water and soil quality because of their sensitive skins, frogs are indicators of the environmental health of waterways. Also because their skins cannot prevent water loss through osmosis, no frogs

Litoria ewingi (Brown tree frog)

the water, usually in spring when flooding creates temporary ponds where eggs can be laid and tadpoles can develop. At various locations on most rivers and especially along their lower reaches when flooded, trout enter marshes and swamps sometimes to forage for frogs. In the river itself, trout look for them in the weedy shallows of backwaters and sidewaters.

Using a living or dead frog for bait has now been banned in Tasmania.

Identifying, often by their calls, the local frogs most likely of interest to trout can help when choosing flies or lures to match their size and colour. An audio cassette titled *Frogs Tasmania: Natural History and Calls* may be helpful. Produced by a northern Tasmanian field naturalists' club, it is available from Launceston's Queen Victoria Museum, Royal Park.

Two of the frogs most common in rivers and lakes throughout the state are the brown tree frog *Litoria ewingi* and the small, inconspicuous common froglet *Crinea signifera*. The first species is of medium size and delicate build, brown on the back and white underneath, is found at all altitudes and breeds in ponds. It calls in and out of water and from trees, mostly at night and

except a crab-eating species in south east Asia can tolerate saltwater. Most frogs are, however, well adapted to uncertain supplies of fresh water, and large populations will survive dry spells hidden away until the rains come. Because frogs will then show up in force, that's one time when trout will be looking for them.

Another is when female frogs are laying eggs in

Crinea signifera (Common froglet)

Limnodynastes tasmaniensis (Spotted marsh frog)

especially after rain, with a long 'whirring' cricket-like 'ree-ree-ree-ree-ree-ree'. The second species is the most abundant and widespread in Tasmania and can breed in shallow, temporary water. It has a brown back sometimes patterned, is white with black blotches below and calls in and out of water, all year and again especially after rain, with a 'craak, craak, craak, craak' rapidly repeated 7 to 15 times.

A third frog, also small and inconspicuous, is the indigenous Tasmanian froglet *Crinia tasmaniensis,* which though not so widespread is common mainly on the Central Plateau and in the north and west of the state beside the running water in which it prefers to breed. Found also in permanent and temporary ponds, it prefers undisturbed habitats to highest altitudes. This froglet is light grey to brown on the back, black and white underneath and the undersides of its thighs and groin can be a brilliant red. It makes in spring and summer, and sometimes in winter, an ususual lamb-like 'baa-aa-aaaa' from the water's edge.

All these frogs lay eggs over much of the year, especially in spring and summer with spring the busiest time. The eggs of the common and Tasmanian froglets are laid in shallow water, singly or sometimes in the case of the latter in small clumps, and sink to the bottom. Those of the brown tree frog are laid in clusters like

bunches of grapes and are wound round the stems of plants. All three frogs share the need to swim out to suitable places and are then vulnerable to trout.

Fish foraging in still, weedy shallows can be expected in spring, especially in the evening and at night. Often cruising very slowly, they sometimes wait for several minutes in ambush and may well find irresistible a large wet fly such as a Yeti, Robin, Muddler Minnow or Mrs Simpson fished just below the surface and twitched back to imitate a swimming frog. Effective where frogs are loud can also be a metal lure like a frog-pattern wobbler, or a rather bushy fly like a Hairy Mary, 'parked' on the surface and twitched under when a trout approaches. Fly fishers can also try attracting a trout's attention by plopping a fly heavily onto the water-especially along sheer banks sheltering deep, slack water.

For anglers on the Central Plateau, who are the ones usually most interested in such fishing, that green and golden frog *Litoria raniformis* which has been in decline may also still be encountered. Three times bigger than the froglets and the largest of all the Tasmanian species, this frog with its green to brown back and white belly prefers ponds, lagoons and large swamps in which to lay its eggs in spring and summer. When the water was high enough, it was in the past attracted to those marshes in some corners of Lake Sorell

which built up a reputation for trout that were actively 'frogging'. The green and golden frog calls in spring and summer from water, with long, modulated 'craw-aw-aw-aw-awk' growls. Its present strongholds appear to be in the north-east of Tasmania, especially in the Blackmans Lagoon area where a thriving population still exists, and the Waterhouse area together with the Deloraine-Launceston-Tamar Valley region.

Other waters highland anglers could investigate are those in the Lake St Clair area which is home to at least four species. The Great Lake hosts many too, especially along its northern shores. The spotted marsh frog *Limnodynastes tasmaniensis* is one species found in other waters on the Plateau, although it is most common on the lowlands in farm dams, temporary creeks, open woodland, coastal wetlands, streams in the state's Midlands and central north and often in floodwaters. Medium in size and white underneath, it has a

grey-brown back with green spots and a yellow to red stripe, and calls from water in spring and summer with a single loud 'ick' like stones being clicked together. Its frothy egg masses are easily recognisable as they float in open water among scattered vegetation.

As well as adult frogs, waters where eggs have been laid also, of course, contain tadpoles. On these, trout often prey: sometimes swirling among weed beds to force them out into the open. Tadpoles will be found in some waters throughout the year but in most waters are most common in spring and to a lesser extent in summer, especially in the highlands where they hatch later in the cooler conditions there.

Weed beds also shelter freshwater shrimps ... and snails. And as detailed at the start of Chapter 1, those same snails can generate memorable angling action- more than just occasionally, for those anglers in the know. While a few species of aquatic snail are omnivorous and feed not

Gyraulus genus, showing the planispiral shell.

only on dead plants but also on dead animals, most species are vegetarian and associated closely with water plants. Snails are rarely found in water low in calcium: they are rare therefore in water usually acid and with the low pH values looked at in more depth in Chapter 8. They are rare also in water organically polluted and in the deeper parts of stillwaters.

There are at least 28 species of freshwater snail in Tasmania, five of them widespread through most of the state's freshwaters with an introduced New Zealand hydrobiid being the most abundant snail in many parts. Snails are of considerable economic interest throughout Australia because one snail, *Lymnaea tomentosa*, is the host for the liver fluke of sheep. This species is rare in the western third of Tasmania but widespread through the rest of the state.

Freshwater snails are relished by trout, especially when they collect in the surface film where they can be gathered with little effort. Snails occasionally rise to the surface when the water warms, perhaps due to the build-up of gas in their shells or because they need more oxygen. Little conical snails will be found coming down at times in lowland rivers whose waters hold sufficient calcium for them, especially when the spring floods which have washed them into newly filled nooks and crannies are receding and the shallows are warming up.

Such shallow corners are often so numerous and small on most of even the larger rivers of natural flow that locating them, and the snails which just sometimes float down from them, is usually difficult-and sometimes made almost by accident, as I've already described. There are some waters, though, such as the artificially boosted Brumbys Creek which receives water from the Great Lake on the plateau high overhead after it has gone through tunnels, pipes then the turbines of the Poatina Power Station, where larger expanses of the one sort of habitat can be found.

In this instance, it should be a large-enough area of weedy flats which is becoming shallower and warmer as the water level falls. At Brumbys, a water half river and half lake, this usually is because a turbine or two has been shut down in the power station. If from that same area only a few major currents flow out, the angler noting sipping rises in them but no obvious items of food on the surface should suspect floating snails-from

now on, along similar parts of flooded major rivers, I will too.

Similarly in stillwaters with large expanses of weedy shallows, such as the major marshes which existed in Lake Sorell, floating snails attract trout when these shallows warm up and an offshore breeze blows briskly enough to nudge snails out from them into water open enough to make it a simple enough matter for trout to rise to them. This may also happen just off swampy shorelines, along which trout may cruise regularly in warmer weather, looking for stick caddis as well as snails.

A small river backwater too weedy for trout to find worms but, as the swirl shows, fine for 'froggers'.

They often find a dry fly acceptable, fortunately so considering how shallow the water often is.

Analysis of my fishing diaries covering 15 seasons shows that snails were inside 48 per cent of the 620 trout caught from Brumbys Creek. They were particularly well represented in spring, fell away somewhat in summer and thickened again in autumn. The tiny, round black snails, probably of the *Gyraulus* genus with coiled flat or planispiral shells, followed a similar pattern in Brumbys to its shrimps: thickest from late winter to early summer when they tailed off to almost

nothing, to reappear in autopsies in mid autumn.

As could be expected, the snails of the lower Macquarie River, which receives much of its water from Brumbys Creek, according to my records were of similar importance to the fish there and appeared in them at similar times of the year. In the middle stretches of the Macquarie above its junction with Brumbys Creek, snails were also staple items of diet and found in 43 per cent of the 691 trout checked, but seemed to be of equal importance over the entire season. Other personal records show that snails have been of much more importance to trout in the slow, weedy lowland rivers such as the Meander and Break O'Day-at least during summer and early autumn when the mayflies hatch and when I therefore made most of the autopsies on lake trout-than to trout in stillwaters on the Central Plateau.

According to the figures published for a limited number of trout waters by Buckney and Tyler in *Chemistry of Tasmanian Inland Waters*, the amount of calcium in the Break O'Day is almost ten times greater than the average for four other northern lowland streams more broken in flow. Interestingly, calcium levels in the one river can sometimes vary widely from one part of it to another, so that the upper South Esk River at Mathinna approximated the low calcium levels of the four broken streams, whereas the lower South Esk at Perth contained three times more. Nor are pH levels related exactly to calcium content, with the pH value measured at Mathinna significantly higher than that at Perth.

Save for isolated exceptions, such as Lagoon of Islands which was on a par with the Break O'Day, calcium levels of most lakes on the Central Plateau were similar to, or less than, those of the broken streams. Nevertheless, snails were still taken avidly when available, being particularly important in the past in Lake Sorell, where a quarter of fish caught when this lake was fishing well had been feeding on them, and at Little Pine Lagoon where they were found in 17 per cent of trout, followed by Arthurs Lake with 14 per cent, and Great Lake where they showed up in only 4 per cent of fish. In Arthurs Lake and Lake Sorell snails were eaten consistently throughout the season, but in Little Pine they peaked in trout at the end of summer, occurring in twice as many fish then as at the beginning. It comes as no surprise to find that calcium levels in Sorell were measured as being almost three times higher than

in Great Lake, with Arthurs halfway between.

Certain freshwater crustacea commonly known as 'shrimps' are important trout food in many of the state's waters. The order Amphipoda is the most heavily represented in Tasmania, and since similar species are known as 'scud' in North America, for the sake of uniformity it seems desirable to further David Scholes' forecast in *Fly-fisher in Tasmania* that both Amphipods and the closely related Isopods will come to be known here by the same name. Going even further, I will also describe as 'scud' the members of the orders Anaspidacea and Decapoda.

My records show that, in contrast with the snails, scud are more popular with trout in stillwaters than in rivers. They showed up in 44 per cent of the 418 trout taken from Little Pine

twice as often as the snails which early in summer had been present in a matching percentage of fish. Snails were of approximately equal importance in both waters, but scud were found in nearly twice as many fish from Little Pine.

In the slow lowland rivers, scud were found in 22 per cent of the trout from Brumbys Creek and were much more important here and in an associated water, the lower Macquarie River, than in the Macquarie above its junction with Brumbys, where they were found in only 4 per cent of fish, not at all after spring and even then entirely absent during half of the 14 seasons analysed. During some autumns they were also scarce in the lower Macquarie.

Waters at different altitudes which, of those checked, seemed most favoured by scud are Little Pine Lagoon in the highlands and Brumbys Creek on the lowlands. In both waters, various sizes of scud were found through spring and summer, which seems to indicate that they continue to breed throughout at least these seasons. Because scud are so important a food for trout in these waters and many others, and because they often stimulate the first angling sport of the new season, further information on them should be of assistance to anglers.

Amphipods have been mentioned already. The adults of their various species range in length from 5 mm to 25 mm and in Tasmania three families are represented: the Ceinidae mostly in still or slow water, the Eusiridae in flowing water and the Gammaridae, which with 25 species is easily the most diverse family. Many Gammarid species are restricted to flowing water and others live mainly in standing fresh water.

Amphipods and Isopods are both orders of the Peracarida division of crustacea, so not surprisingly they look like each other in many ways. Each species of both orders has no carapace, or 'shell', covering all or parts of the body, but features a distinct

Lagoon over 16 seasons in the recent past and were particularly common early in summer when they were in five times more trout than were snails. At the end of summer both scud and snails were almost equally represented, although the ratio overall showed scud in five Little Pine fish compared with snails in two.

Scud were even more important in Great Lake, being found in 48 per cent of trout. Of Lake Sorell trout, 28 per cent contained scud compared with 24 per cent with snails, but the difference was more marked at Arthurs Lake: 25 per cent to 14 per cent. Interestingly, in contrast to Little Pine they appeared most frequently in trout from Arthurs from mid-summer to its end, occurring

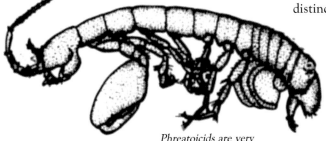

Phreatoicids are very common in Tasmania.

FINDING TROUT

head and seven pairs of walking legs on the thorax or 'chest'. During the breeding season females form, through the growth of overlapping plates on some of the front legs, a brood pouch below the thorax in which eggs hatch directly into tiny adults. The bodies of both Amphipods and Isopods are flattened sideways, with Amphipods usually more strongly compressed. Amphipods also have gills, which are sac-like or branched structures, associated with their thoracic legs rather than with their abdominal appendages, where the gills of Isopods are found. Amphipods use these appendages only for swimming, which they do with a facility unmatched by Isopods.

Species of the order Decapoda, of the separate division Eucarida, are also excellent swimmers. Many species of these crayfish/shrimp type of Decapods, with five pairs of thoracic legs as their name suggests, very prominent carapaces, obvious heads and eyes on stalks, are true shrimps while some others are crabs. Members of the genus *Paratya*, of the family Atydidae, are typical of most of these shrimps in being almost transparent and quick moving. Found usually on the lowlands in small creeks, along the edges of small lakes and hill lakes such as Leake, Sorell and Crescent, they especially like large, slow-flowing or still pools in rivers and congregate under banks, under submerged rocks and among weedbeds. Trout actively chase them as they chase the Amphipods.

The Parastacidae family of Decapods includes the well-known yabbies or freshwater crayfish. Of the ten Australian genera, Tasmania has four. A good deal larger and more robust than other Decapods, yabbies favour small creeks and lowland stillwaters. Many species breed mainly in spring and build burrows as retreats into which they crawl for shelter-sometimes not fast enough to escape the trout of Brumbys Creek, prowling over ground newly covered when extra turbines begin operating in the power station upstream.

Because they can move by no other means than crawling, Isopods are attractively vulnerable to trout. Members of at least two other families of this order live in streams and stillwaters in Tasmania, but most species of Australian Isopods are relatively rare except for those of the Phreatoicidae family, very common in Tasmania and much more common than previously thought. Indeed Phreatoicids live in almost every body of fresh water, typically lakes, dams, swamps and streams of every size. They also favour rotting timber detritus, and for this reason were common in shoreline shallows when higher levels on waters such as Great Lake, Little Pine Lagoon and Lake King William drowned bushes and trees.

Fly fishers should carry nymphs coloured olive to blackish green, weighted and unweighted and in a good range of sizes. Since Amphipods swim with bodies almost straight, such a nymph in lighter green and twitched slowly through the water will imitate them as well. Also successful has been a fly tied on a size 12 up-eyed hook with a curved shank. This fly has a thorax of dark brown seals fur or substitute, beard hackle the same colour and body of green seals fur, taken round the hook bend then ribbed with fine copper wire. The fly may be taken as it falls through the water or lies inert on the bottom. If not, it should be retrieved in slow twitches.

One final scud of importance also favours rotting timber detritus. It has a body 20 mm long with a distinctive and prominent flexure upward half way along it, which makes it look like a little boomerang in shape. Known also as the Great Lake shrimp, this is the single species of the Paranaspides genus, which belongs to the order Anaspidacea of the separate division Syncarida. It has no carapace and, like the Amphipods and Isopods, has a thorax and abdomen which look much the same as each other. Paranaspides scud are found on the bottom of Great Lake, Shannon Lagoon and Penstock Lagoon, waters where not only scud but fish in the shape of little native galaxiids are important to trout.

Typical Paratya Decapod

Chapter 5

Trout Food - Fish

Small fish will interest a feeding trout to a greater or lesser degree depending on how much energy it has to use to secure them. If a smaller fish, made vulnerable perhaps by injury, is big enough to make a meaty mouthful, it will provide a good return on energy invested, be the predator shark or trout. Indeed, as trout grow larger many tend to feed almost exclusively on fish when they are available.

Attractive as usual, both locally and in many other parts of the world, are concentrations of these smaller fish. In the island state of Tasmania, spring fishing of major importance to many anglers has involved resident brown trout, and those 'sea runners' attracted in from the sea, feeding in coastal estuaries on the little fish collectively called whitebait.

Unfortunately, some decades ago the heavy runs of whitebait into major rivers especially along the state's northwest coast were reduced to a trickle by ruthless commercial netting of hundreds of tonnes of them each year. In spite of severe restrictions which have included closed seasons, their numbers are still relatively low. To compensate in a small way, a relatively new fishery has developed in Launceston, thanks to whitebait being attracted from the Tamar by fresh water from the Trevallyn power station flowing

strongly down the tailrace into it. Many anglers have been pleased that access to this tailrace from land has also been much improved in recent years.

Elsewhere along the north coast, a spill of chemicals into the Great Forester River in the recent past certainly slowed sport there but interesting fishing has still been possible in spring on other rivers such as the Leven and the Forth. Sport is more reliable near mouths of streams in the far northwest and along the west coast where exploitation did not occur or was not so severe. Productive rivers in this area include the Henty and Little Henty, the Pieman and Gordon. In the south, the Huon, and the Derwent particularly in the upper half of its estuary, often fish well in spring.

Thanks to the work of scientists such as past Commissioner of Tasmanian Inland Fisheries Wayne Fulton, author of *Tasmanian Freshwater Fishes,* much is now known about the baitfish which are important to Tasmanian trout. Pictures and details are also available by searching for 'Tasmanian native fish' on www.tas.gov.au.

A number of different species make up the whitebait runs. Most important is the Tasmanian whitebait *Lovettia sealii,* followed by jollytail, *Galaxias maculatus,* which is

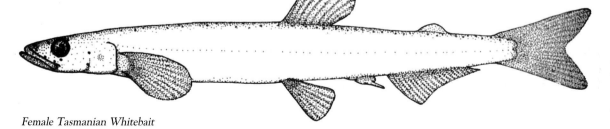

Female Tasmanian Whitebait

Worth the sunburn ...

Oscar Kehrberg plays a hefty brown trout hunting golden galaxias G. auratus along a shallow, rocky shoreline of Kermodes Bay, Lake Sorell.

Oscar Kehrberg nets the weighty fish.

also found in South America and is the major species in New Zealand runs. Also important are the spotted galaxias *G. truttaceus*, the Tasmanian mudfish *G. cleaveri* and the climbing galaxias *G. brevipinnis*. Their juveniles all swim down to the sea, to return in spring. *Lovettia sealii* return to spawn in the lower reaches of coastal rivers at the limit of tidal influence. Before they die, they lay eggs on structures submerged in the water like fallen trees and rocks. Other species return to adult habitats farther up rivers, which in the case of *G. truttaceus* and *G. brevipinnis* may be some distance upstream, with the latter thought to live in the upper reaches of streams.

If fish in the schools are numerous enough, such runs may attract trout into following them well upstream, especially in rivers of uninterrupted flow such as the Leven. Most feeding, though, seems to occur in the brackish water of the lower reaches of coastal rivers. Farther upstream the galaxias change colour to become brown, green or black with paler bellies, but the juveniles are transparent, elongated little fish, about 5 cm in length, as is *Lovettia sealii* which appears to predominate in earlier spring runs and whose silvery sides help camouflage it by reflecting the colours of the water and bottom. First runs of Lovettia seem to attract mainly resident brown trout in some rivers while the genuine, silvery sea-run trout wait for the larger fish in later runs.

Obviously the angler needs imitations like small silver wobblers or large, pale wet flies tied with flash and translucence in mind. Sometimes both are used, with fly droppers rigged in tandem with hardware. Although using fish as bait in Tasmania is now restricted to waters subject to tidal influences, actual baitfish such as little freshwater flathead and prettyfish are still frequently cast out in estuaries, fished on the bottom or unweighted, to be slowly retrieved. When a fish takes, all pressure is removed as soon as possible and the

Spotted galaxias

angler allows the fish to run with the bait before tightening up. Places popular with trout are where the whitebait collect, such as close to any channels or gutters of deeper water, below obstructions like major rapids or a weir, in a resting lie of slower water among or beside the ripples of less rapid flow in particular where river meets estuary and along the edges of vegetation, especially when the water is high. Trout will often remain quietly near the bank until sufficient whitebait congregate *and* will also wait in the slack water below a rocky point for the little fish

the lure to flutter through the shoal and down below it.

Though opinions vary on the most suitable tides for galaxias, one on the way out would seem best for fishing a resting lie as well as a rocky point, and is popular with many recreational netters licensed to take limited numbers of whitebait because, in persuading the little fish to choose slower bankside water, out-going currents bring them within reach from the land. Individual stream contours will determine exactly where to fish on which tides. *Lovettia sealii* differ in having

English perch (redfin)

skirting it to slow and pack together as they fight against the current.

Out they then rush, sending some of the little fish flying into the air in fright. Because chasing fish uses up much energy, trout return to quieter water to conserve energy and to allow it to build up for the next charge. They also prefer prey which looks vulnerable or isolated, usually fish on the edges of a tightly packed shoal. This plainly is where the angler's lure should be, and preferably moving away from the other fish. If trout charge into the shoal itself, it may then be better to allow

a distinct preference for tides, moving upstream as they flow inward and dropping back as they ebb. What anglers do agree on is that low light at dawn or dusk is a good time, as it is also for other fussy trout. For these fish are often very difficult to interest.

Although speed in getting lure to trout and pulling it fast across the noses of feeders chasing shoals on the move is sometimes needed, it is not as critical as it can be in other situations. More often called for is precise casting to fish watching what is sometimes quite a restricted area. As could be expected, a lure which flutters down through the water in between short darts forward will certainly suggest a vulnerable, crippled fish and lures in various weights are needed to counter various speeds of current. Persistence is usually required and visitors with a timetable also need a little luck since floodwaters will slow down the whitebait runs and reduce chances to fish to trout seen feeding. But the rewards are considerable: strong, silvery trout, of good size and in excellent condition.

Small fish are also at times important trout food

spite of some quite frenzied feeding, these trout moving without pattern are hard to interest.

Furthermore, when they do chase they seem to 'lock in' on one specific little fish, and again persistence is required if the lure is eventually to become the target. So it can be with fish feeding on the native galaxias, as I've found out in fishing Curries River Dam, a lowland lagoon in the central north not far from Bass Strait. Trout in a couple of patches were feeding spasmodically in open water, each slashing and boiling three or four times in lines and arcs just below the surface.

Western paragalaxias

inland. While the climbing and spotted galaxias are numerous in parts of some rivers, the trout of the stillwaters are usually those that feed not only on galaxias but also on redfin, the English perch *Perca fluviatilis*. Late in spring, perch eggs hatch into small, silvery fry in the slower rivers and in stillwaters such as Lake Echo, Lake Leake, Dee Lagoon and Lagoon of Islands, where they shoal for some time before becoming solitary. Large schools usually swim near the surface and well out from shore, where trout feed on them with slashes and swirls. As may be expected, and in

They were hunting little fish which were probably spotted galaxias, although three other species are also found here. No confirmation was possible because I could manage only a couple of nips to a green nymph and a damselfly dry, flies whose diversity indicates the desperation of the angler as well as the flightiness of the fish.

Spotted galaxias, with orange to red fins and body colours which range from brown with black spots to black all over, are also quite widespread on the Central Plateau, in Great Lake and the western lakes. The climbing galaxias, greyish

Golden galaxias

brown to dark olive on the back, paler on the sides and with a dull silvery-olive belly, is a species even more widespread due to its astonishing ability to climb very high falls-and even damp rock faces-using its large pectoral and pelvic fins. It is found not only together with spotted galaxias but also in Lakes Echo, St Clair, King William, Pedder and Gordon. Lures based on these descriptions need to be fished deep because both species prefer to live beneath or among cover on the beds of these lakes.

Other species, however, are not only restricted to a much more limited area but also prefer the rocky margins of stillwaters rather than their beds. An exception is the Great Lake paragalaxias *Paragalaxias eleotroides*, a small fish only 5.5 cm long with golden brown back, pale yellow or white belly and clear golden fins. Also found in the Shannon and Penstock Lagoons, it is more common deep down. In the same waters, the Shannon paragalaxias *P. dissimilis* prefers the rocky edges where it spawns in summer. Dark grey to black on back and sides, grey white underneath and with clear fins, this fish at 7.5 cm is a little longer than its relative.

The western paragalaxias *P. julianus* is found in the western lakes drained by the upper reaches of the Pine, James and Ouse Rivers, specifically as its name suggests, in the Julian lakes and in Pillans, Ball and Silver to name a few others. It grows to

Arthurs paragalaxias

10 cm in length, is dark brown to black on top with dark blotches on its grey sides and has clear fins.

In Arthurs and Woods Lakes two native species exist, and like *P. julianus* both prefer rocky edges. The Arthurs paragalaxias *P. mesotes* is dark green to grey on the back, with similar patches on its pale yellow sides. the belly is pale yellow, the fins are clear and the fish grow to a length of at least 8 cm. The other species is the saddled galaxias *Galaxias tanycephalus*, with dark green back, yellow green sides and silver belly. This fish grows to 15 cm and although the larger ones have black

the Silver Plains marshes and around Grassy Point. Some have also been found in the past near weed along the front of various marshes where these meet the lake proper.

In the main, however, anglers should seek out and watch rocky edges for the feeding trout which will sometimes be signalled by galaxias flying out of the water like whitebait. One fishery where this sight has been seen more often in recent springs is Tooms Lake, in eastern Tasmania. Trout seem to chase the little fish towards the shore, as they do at times in Curries River Dam, then

Rocky shore of a Julians Lake, habitat for Paragalaxias julianus.

backs and sides and grey bellies, it is not surprising that lures coloured green and gold are so popular in Arthurs and Woods Lakes.

The golden galaxias *G. auratus* live in Lake Sorell and Lake Crescent. Golden amber in colour, with dark spots on sides and back and with fins amber to light orange, they too prefer rocky margins but are also found, in Lake Sorell and especially in spring, over the beds of pebbles to be found near Kermodes Bay, to the south of

retreat to deeper water where they will sometimes wait, resting and on watch, before charging again. Sport becomes a matter of the angler finding and concentrating on a likely spot, then timing the charges so that the lure can be set out just before the next is due and twitched upward when the trout shows. A fly is obviously best for this and an alternative to an orthodox large wet is one just bushy enough to float awash until, as for froggers, it is twitched under when a trout draws nigh.

Chapter 6
Trout Senses

A trout uses its senses to protect itself and to obtain food. It becomes aware of prey often through sight, sometimes through smell, hearing or the use of its lateral line, and gathers that food using its vision.

The sense of smell is exceptionally keen in a salmon, good enough for it to recognise the characteristic smell of the stream where it was hatched and to home in on it from out at sea. Sea trout may well share some of this endowment, and following research in New Zealand, scientists announced in 1997 that a magnetic sensor found in the noses of rainbow trout may help explain how many animals navigate over long distances. Although the lobe of a freshwater trout's brain which deals with smell is small and poorly developed compared with the lobe looking after sight, a trout still has a well-developed sense of smell and is probably able to detect different odours. The trout does have on each side of its snout the twin-nostril system which allows water to flow into the front nostril and out the rear and which is more efficient than the single nostril of other types of fish.

Smell may be used to become aware of food at night and when vision is reduced by clouded water, typically during floods. When other food is not available, the possibility that moving water may dissipate the odour of terrestrial food such as drowned worms may explain why trout are almost never found feeding in it during floods. Knowing their preference for still water when a river breaks its banks, especially early in the season when other kinds of food are not yet about, will save the angler many fruitless hours checking flowing water, even though the current in it may be a lazy one. Even in places like old river courses, flowing

only during floods, trout will still fossick in corners and along edges where there are no currents.

A trout hears using the inner ears which also enable it to maintain its balance. Though the fish cannot hear sounds in the air unless they are accompanied by vibrations from ground to water, sounds in the water itself are transmitted directly through its head to the ears. Sound travels very much better through water than through air and, since fish in trouble give off distinctive vibrations

Trout see better in the oily water along this sheltered shore of Arthurs Lake.

of distress, is important to trout in warning them of danger. Knowing this, the angler who has just landed a fish should either try somewhere else some distance away or wait for the neighbours to calm down.

The noise of tail thumps and surface splashes made when feeding may also alert trout that something like a hatch is on and by prompting all of them to start rising together, account for the strange phenomenon of a whole long stretch of water appearing to come alive at once. Although a trout uses its eyes for the final chase, hearing like smell also seems to alert it to the presence in the general area of prey such as baitfish splashing in the shallows at night, and the angler's lure which also splashes when it lands may well arouse interest.

Ears are needed to detect higher-frequency sounds and sounds made more than about six metres away. An important supplementary organ, however, is the lateral line which most fish possess in one form or another. In a trout, it is a delicate

Ray Klimeck with a brown in good condition from Gunns Lake-shown behind, and not much deeper anywhere at the time.

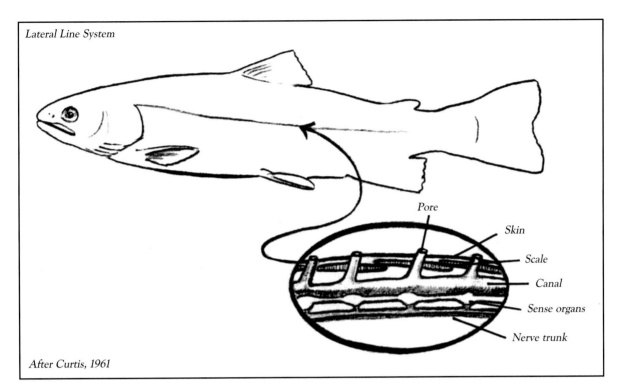

Lateral Line System

Pore

Skin

Scale

Canal

Sense organs

Nerve trunk

After Curtis, 1961

line which runs down each side and is made up of a series of canals just under the skin containing sensory cells activated by vibrations reaching them through thousands of openings. Vibrations which can be detected are those made by disturbances close by which create sound waves of low frequency, such as the movements of baitfish, or of lures imitating them. Described by some as 'the sense of distant touch', the lateral line can sense the course and distance of prey like baitfish up to six metres away, and pinpoint them with exactitude if they come within a metre of it.

The smaller fish, however, has the advantage of its own lateral line's superiority in detecting the larger trout sooner, an advantage which can be offset by the trout's use of its most important sense, vision.

In preferring to feed early and late in the day, trout not only take advantage of their vision adapting more efficiently to low light levels than the vision of their prey, but also at these times are more willing to risk increased danger to themselves by cruising in shallower water because the eyes of many of their own predators do not adapt as well either.

Trout rely extensively on their vision to find and gather food, and as already outlined for specific items of their prey, they very much favour places where their eyes operate best. When light enters water, a surface ruffled by current, or more commonly wind, will break it up and reflect much of it back to the sky. Trout look for a smooth surface partly because they can more easily spot insects floating or landing on it and can see through it better.

Using the superior distance perception of its binocular vision-the independent vision of each eye overlaps dead ahead of it to provide a narrow band of about 40 degrees of stereoscopic sight-the fish is even able to track flies on the wing and to jump with astonishing precision at them. Since binocular vision is so important to them trout may well use it most of the time, and as David Scholes points out in *Trout and Trouting*, objects within range of their monocular vision may be in sight but may not register in their conscious awareness. Such objects may need to move to be noticed by the fish.

With more light reaching the bottom through a smooth surface, the search for food like snails and scud among the weeds is easier. Trout often seem to stop 'tailing' when the surface becomes ruffled and visibility decreases. Occasionally they continue to feed with reduced zeal and may be hidden by the disturbed surface, but much more often they actually stop feeding altogether and

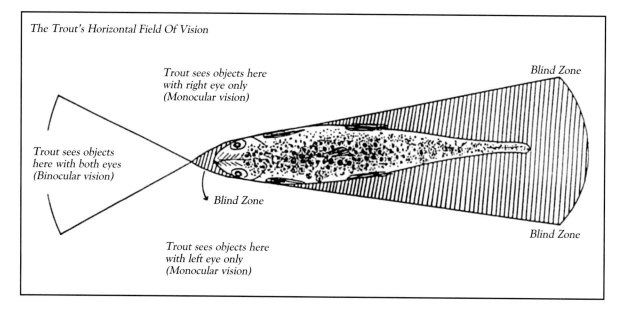

The Trout's Horizontal Field Of Vision

Trout sees objects here
with right eye only
(Monocular vision)

Blind Zone

Trout sees objects
here with both eyes
(Binocular vision)

Blind Zone

Blind Zone

Trout sees objects here
with left eye only
(Monocular vision)

either wait for the wind to ease, or move elsewhere. Another advantage of a very smooth surface is that it is partially a mirror and in shallow water fish can see the bottom reflected in it together with prey or predators hiding, perhaps on the other side of a rock and not visible directly through the water.

If the wind does start blowing, the angler can

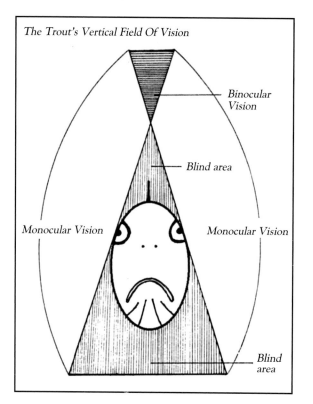

The Trout's Vertical Field Of Vision

Binocular
Vision

Blind area

Monocular Vision

Monocular Vision

Blind
area

find an unruffled 'top' by choosing to visit a water protected by hills or bush, or in the case of much of the St Patricks River in northern Tasmania, by both. In the highlands, the Pine Tier Dam is almost completely protected by hills, and sheltered parts can be found on many other stillwaters such as lakes Leake and Sorell, Arthurs and Great lakes and Dee and Penstock lagoons where oily water behind shelter encourages trout to gather and remain within range of an angler on shore.

Tactically, if a wind blows up suddenly on more exposed water such as a river of the meadows, smooth patches can often be found in the lee of trees like willows and at the foot of the higher banks mentioned in the first two chapters. More extensive slicks form in front of natural embankments and lines of trees, often planted in shelter-belts. Knowing the location of such places and the direction of the wind will often enable a good choice of venue to be made before even setting off from home.

For fly fishers, however, there is another side to this matter of wind which I was to find out on a visit to the lower Macquarie River.

The afternoon hadn't started well: only twenty steps and over I went, tripping in a drainage ditch and filling my body waders with bracing water from the Great Lake.

Thankfully, dry clothes were close by in the jeep, but changing into them wasn't made easier by the crispness of autumn-nor by a breeze just starting to blow from the north-west, already ruffling the river's surface, and freshening...

Was fishing really worth the candle today? Here it was mid-April and only a fortnight of Tasmania's brown trout season left, not much insect food about, and only musty old clothes to wear. Home, picking a few late blackberries on the way?

After so recently opening them, perhaps it was the thought of those farm gates facing me before the easy half hour drive north to Launceston. More likely it was simply that mulishness I'm sure I share, practically I suppose by definition, with most other trouters. For whatever reason, I emptied water from my fly boxes, noting glumly in doing so that the only one to remain dry held my wet flies, festooned the jeep with soggy apparel, pulled on my leg waders...and doggedly set off downriver again.

Two days ago, my trip in full sunshine to this big trout stream, filled as it usually is in most autumns with cool, crystal-clear water, had involved feverishly covering trout sipping spasmodically at something or other on or near the surface, or jumping now and then in the flat calm to mayfly spinners.

No wind when mayflies are about nearly always means that a fly fisher's most wishful prayer has been answered...but on this occasion, each cast resulted only in every fish promptly 'going down as though pole-axed', as a mate would say (expletive deleted), and just one small brownie had finally sucked in the Brown Dun I was using to prospect deep, knotted water along one sheer bank edged with tussocks.

Things had looked promising for the first few hours of that trip, but weren't. Today, chances of sport seemed slim right from the start.

Granted, this part of the Macquarie, about 19 river kilometres long and immediately above its junction with the South Esk River at Longford, was still running a banker-thanks to all the highland water from the Poatina hydro station feeding into it near Cressy via Brumbys Creek. The air did feel reasonably warm, especially when the sun occasionally broke through, and at least the wind was blowing off my bank and not onto it.

Unfortunately, that breeze was steadily growing stronger, and I hadn't seen or heard any fish feeding in the ripple. And so far the only insects on the water had been one or two grasshoppers, to windward of a couple of patches where they had remained reasonably thick, plus a few more of those mayflies-but today only solitary, windblown

duns, fluttering across the surface every ten minutes or so, not often enough to attract any swallows.

Nevertheless, towards the end of previous seasons here, duns just like these had sparked gratifying sport from brownies well aware of the closeness of spawning and winter, and keen to feed. So I tied on a favourite Brown Dun, and started to prospect, systematically but without much hope, up a straight of faster flow which had often been productive in other autumns.

This 300-metre stretch was wide, and from my bank to the deep central channel its richly-weeded bed shelved gently from thigh to chest deep: deep

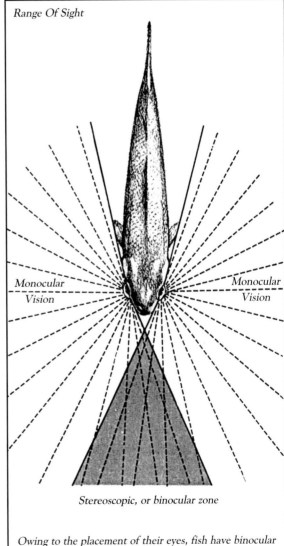

Range Of Sight

Monocular Vision

Monocular Vision

Stereoscopic, or binocular zone

Owing to the placement of their eyes, fish have binocular vision only in a small area in front of them. Each eye, however, can scan an arc of 180 degrees to the side.

enough for trout to feel secure, shallow enough for them to easily see and come up for tucker on top. And down the stretch flowed currents of good speed too: slow enough for trout to hold comfortably, brisk enough to force them into sometimes over-hasty judgments about that tucker drifting down.

Drifting down right now with a regularity disturbingly unbroken was my size 14 floater with its single, sloping, light brown wing, brown and grey seal's fur body and sparse hackles, black in front of brown. But it was hard to spot on that wind-roughened surface, and thinking that the trout might be having the same problem, I changed to a more substantial and buoyant size 12 dun-one of my smaller lake flies, in fact.

Not long after, a trout boiled at the larger dun when I was about to recast. This was promising- the fish had risen quite close to me, and nothing like that had happened two days before. And yet it had still shied away at the last moment...

Standing shin deep in weed and water, I went on covering the water above: one cast a metre or so out from my low bank, another a couple of metres out from that, another along the edge of the heavily-ruffled water where the wind struck the flow fair and square. Shuffle up half a dozen steps and repeat, watching that little brown dot closely, knowing full well that the instant the eyes strayed from it was the very same instant that a fish would take.

That little fly bobbing down towards me had become the only thing that mattered. Casting grew mechanical, the whole process almost spellbinding- fine if you had troubles to forget, not so good if angling action was the aim. After a further half hour of fruitless searching, I stopped casting to give the matter some serious thought.

A trout had been interested enough to rise and to at least look closely at the fly; because of that and the clearness of the water, I decided to change the tippet from three kilogram thickness to two kilos rather than trying another dun, or a grasshopper tie.

Only a couple of fish showed in the ripple, each chopping once probably at skittering duns. Yet it wasn't long before an unseen brownie took with a chonk-only half a kilo, but it battled hard in the brisk flow and jumped high several times. Soon after, an unlucky fish decided to gulp the Dun down just as I was lifting it off to recast and was probably just as surprised as I. This trout, and

Stretch of lower Macquarie River referred to, of suitable flow topped by just enough of a ripple to make a floater effective.

another which took quietly close to the bank near the top of the straight, were twice as big as the first, but like it were short and deep-and very strong.

Each fish was also hooked hard in a corner of the mouth, in 'the scissors'. Thanks perhaps to wind ruffling the surface and reducing their vision, it seemed that at least some of the trout so fussy in the flat calm two days ago had been forced to stop gazing about, to pay closer attention to their own little patches-and to any likely-looking morsels floating over them.

After going on so many fishing trips, it strikes me that each is always a mixture of the good and the bad, of pleasure and disappointment in varying degrees. And although reminding myself of this at the top of the straight, after having left that good little Brown Dun in a very nice trout which had lifted a large head over the fly just after it lit on the water, my lack of control in striking the best fish of the day too hard still rankled.

The wind strengthened too, enough indeed to blow me back to the jeep and away. Nevertheless, I drove home pleased; the trip may have started

and ended badly, but there'd been good sport in between, I'd collected a few pleasant memories to help get me through another winter-and I'd learnt that in some conditions wind can be a blessing instead of a curse.

Water clarity is important because it affects how much light actually penetrates through the water itself and therefore also affects how well a fish can see. Particles of silt scatter and block the light so that, in spite of its noted ability to see in the dimness, in heavily coloured water trout may not have time to react, chase and then swallow faster-

The vision of trout in the little St Patricks River is rarely diminished by too much wind.

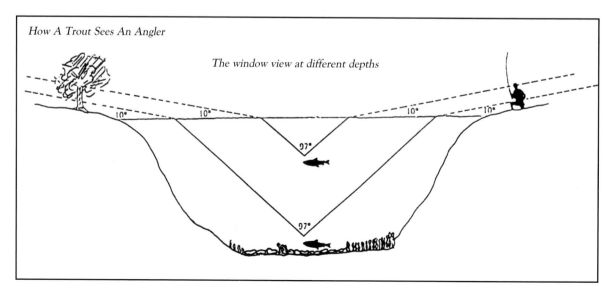

How A Trout Sees An Angler

The window view at different depths

moving prey such as baitfish or their imitations before the gloom does it for them. Even during the hatch of mayflies on the flat rivers in spring with trout expecting and actively looking for them, dirty water and only a few flies equate to one of the very few certainties concerning trout activity: there won't be any.

Fortunately, rarely do all rivers become unfishable at the same time and anglers visiting the highlands can avoid the stillwaters mentioned in the first chapter. Yet even on smaller, shallower lagoons with muddy beds such as Penstock, and Little Pine when its level has dropped, areas where feeder streams enter are usually worth checking for the clearer water which can also often be found in other corners, shores and bays if enough distance is covered. Similarly, unless exceptional run-off has brought in just too much silt, on moving water there will be backwaters and sidewaters just off the main flow where vegetation like spike-rushes seems to filter out some of it and where the water is clearer. In the Macquarie and most other rivers trout frequently stay near the main channels unless better pickings are available elsewhere, but in a few others such as Brumbys Creek, as a matter of course they range and feed freely through the slower, clearer water.

One particular sort of river backwater popular with trout in times of flood is the one described by experienced local angler Len Smith as a 'light globe', after its shape of single narrow opening widening into a basin. With no flow through them, fish seem to prefer these 'light globes' as refuges where respiration is easier and so is finding by sight and smell drowned morsels such as worms.

Trout vision is affected by water depth, and when looking for feeders during floods anglers should concentrate more on water no deeper than a metre. Trout peering into weedbeds for creatures like small scud and snails also welcome better vision in the shallows where light is stronger. Examples are weeds covered in spring by water usually high then on Tasmania's Central Plateau. Places to check include parts of the nearer western lakes such as those beside the Little Pine River just before it enters Lake Kay, and areas where water barely covers the bands of weedbeds which grow in Great Lake along shorelines protected from the wave action caused by the strong westerly winds which prevail on the Central Plateau. When this lake falls to a level low enough, productive beds of weeds such as those around Tods Corner are nearer both the surface and the shore and can be prospected by fish and wading angler alike. Similarly, weedy runs in lowland rivers are worth checking when there is enough water over them to make trout feel secure but not enough to spoil their vision.

Although a trout's vision is not as sharp as our own and it cannot see much detail at a distance over about five metres, there seems little doubt that its vision and perception of detail out to a metre are excellent. To repeat, conclusive evidence of this is a trout's ability to secure with consistency flies on the wing some distance above the water.

A fish is naturally short-sighted because its eyes are round rather than flattened like ours. It can in fact focus on distant objects by using a retractor muscle in each eye to move the lens closer to the retina. As sight feeders trout can do this very well, but as in other fish, when the muscle is at rest the lens is set for the excellent close-up vision which is vital to concluding the chase or harvest to its satisfaction.

The liking trout have for feeding by sight in shallow water enables anglers to both spot their movements more easily and to remain more often unnoticed themselves. Focusing by the fish at such short range means that distracting, extraneous objects such as lines and leaders will not be noticed. Anglers speak of fishing without problems in water 30 cm deep to trout taking flies floating on crystal-clear highland tarns but of frightening the same fish in water only 20 or 30 cm deeper. This can be put down to trout diving deeper between takes, using a longer focus to spot the next fly, and so being more likely to notice the angler or gear, especially if either is moving. Some small highland stillwaters, such as Gunns Lake just to the north of Arthurs Lake, can indeed become so shallow that their trout simply cannot go deeper and cautious anglers can wade very close to them.

Refraction can be a problem. Rays of light passing from the air to a denser medium such as water are bent, or refracted and in practical terms this means that the trout sees the angler on the bank or in a boat much more often than vice versa. Within reason, the deeper the fish lies the more it can see out of the water, whereas a trout both near the surface and also focusing on flies only a few centimetres away, like tiny caenid mayflies coming down on the current, can often be unaware when feeding hard of an angler only a few metres away.

Fish from one of the western lakes, Howes Lagoon Bay, and the sheltering rocks from where they came.

Chapter 7

Trout Comfort - Shelter

In the trout's continual struggle to keep body and soul together vision is vital in finding food, but even more fundamental to its well-being is the ability to avoid predators and find suitable shelter from them. Shelter from the sun, silt and currents are other factors influencing its comfort, together with suitable temperature and enough oxygen.

Anglers looking to find the feeding lies of trout need to bear in mind at all times the overriding importance to them of security from predation. This will often decide the position of their holding lies and nearly always will also be an important consideration for them when feeding. Even when in shallow water, trout-as outlined in the previous chapter-use to advantage their superior vision in dim light to cruise there usually early and late in the day, except at rare times when much easy food such as a heavy hatch of duns causes a feeding frenzy or, in occupying a water uniformly shallow, they have no choice in the matter.

In open, shallow, silty waters such as O'Dells Lake on the Central Plateau, trout use for shelter banks undercut by wave and runnel action, to the extent that anglers sometimes cannot see trout because they are standing on them! In waters uniform except for areas of rocks, like Howes Lagoon Bay, trout shelter among these, and if no fish are showing this is where the angler should try first. Weedbeds as in Penstock and Little Pine Lagoons serve the same purpose, and when small stillwaters like Gunns Lake fall to shin depth, trout will occupy depressions among clumps of weeds.

Although some trout in shallower streams will shelter in faster water below its ruffled surface, if there are depths others will often hold close to them. The wading angler at Lake Rowallan may find more action fishing lures not over the south-western shallows but among the dead trees in the northwest where the course of the drowned Mersey River runs close to shore. Where shallow water covers a shelf or ledge which drops rapidly away to deeper water, the edge of this 'drop-off' is an excellent place to try, and memories of edges around Great Lake, such as at Cramps Bay, and at Arthurs along the shore between the pumphouse and Hydro Bay readily spring to mind.

On rivers, feeding lies may be in shallower water but those of the bigger trout are often also near the deeper pools. On the Break O'Day River halfway between Fingal and St Marys, a shallow glide with a bed of bare clay is popular with some good trout, especially when mayflies hatch and die in several fertile reaches immediately upstream. These fish are then clearly visible lying over the clay as they take the spent spinners coming down, but only a metre or two below them is a large, dark and very deep hole.

As well as beds of weeds growing near the bottom and trees overhead deterring predators, other vegetation can also provide shelter from them. As mentioned in the first chapter, the fleshy spike-rushes which grow close together in thick bands in the slower lowland rivers like the Macquarie form little bays and pockets where fish lie, often next to nice, strong currents which bring food right to the doors of their snug shelters.

In the upper weir of Brumbys Creek, large willows continue to grow on the banks of the original creek, now flooded by waters from the Poatina Power Station. A number of factors combine with the willows to favour the trout: surrounded by weedy shallows and with the depths of the old creek close handy, good fish live under their protective canopies which reach down to brush the water. These trees are bordered by numerous currents, some of which flow directly under them. Other currents run close by along the edges of the smooth water which is to be found on most days between the trees and the newer banks, no matter how strong the wind. Brown trout lie or cruise slowly along the arc where branches meet slicks, looking for food on or at times above the surface. Like Little Pine Lagoon fish, many are big and knowing-and as for a southern shore of Little Pine, this area has also come to be known as 'The Untouchables'.

Such trees also provide shelter from a bright sun, as they do on smaller rivers like the North Esk where trout will sometimes rise only in slow runs and pools heavily shaded. While this applies especially in summer, at any time of the season when water is high enough to spill into billabongs, fish cruising and 'mooching about' in them value the shelter provided by surrounding willows-as I was to find out at first hand one mid-autumn day.

I'd been around a variety of northern Tasmanian rivers near Launceston, hoping to locate moving trout in them but finding each one 'out of order'. Following heavy, localised rain, Brumbys Creek was running muddy and low; the wee Lake River was reasonably clear but high now; the lower Macquarie which received the flow of both was muddy and high, while in contrast at Stewarton the middle Macquarie, flowing down from the eastern hills where no rain had fallen, continued to be simply too low and too clear for trout to dare show themselves in the full light of day, in spite of handsome clouds of spinners and damselflies over it.

Hoping against hope, I arrived on the upper reaches of the North Esk in mid afternoon, only too aware of the rain clouds low overhead, their gloom matching my mood. But lo! While the little stream did run quite strongly it was not far above summer level, its water was beautifully unsullied...and a fish moved in the deep, dark pool at the bridge-only a couple of times, yet promising nonetheless. But nothing else showed as I trudged down to the last real hope: a small billabong among the willows which just might hold enough water to interest an adventurous trout or two.

My heart sank upon arrival at its lower end. As usual, there was quite a brisk flow down it but today the clear water was only shin deep, apart

from a few gutters where it might reach the knees. But wait, over there in the gloom near the other bank only a few steps away, wasn't that a swirl? In the South Esk at such a low height, it could have been made by a redfin perch-but not here, surely not, I thought. Besides, and hard below, isn't that another fish which has just gulped something down from the current? Surely they're both trout...

Indeed they were, and even though I had to wade out noisily through the silt to the front of the fringing willows to get in any sort of half-decent cast, the trout across from me continued to patrol deliberately around its little pocket of still water on the other side of the flow-though the fish below,

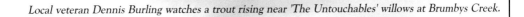
Local veteran Dennis Burling watches a trout rising near 'The Untouchables' willows at Brumbys Creek.

perhaps looking upstream in checking the current, had gone quiet and very likely had seen me standing in full view in the water with a willow at my back.

Out went my small Red Tag floater, only size 15 but with good hackle heavily oiled: certainly needed in this situation where the main aim of getting it across under the willows and somewhere near that trout a mere 5 metres away took precedence over any delicacy in its delivery. Flip after side-arm flip I made, cutting short the backcasts to miss the willows behind, holding my breath each time and fleetingly grateful that the weight of the number 6 fly line was loading the rod

enough to make possible these short, aerial roll-casts and that, while the fly was certainly not alighting like thistledown, at least the Ritz-tapered leader was uncurling well enough to put it down reasonably gently onto the far side of the flow.

Time after time I followed the float of that tiny red dot. The trout ignored it and me, continuing to feed-but not from the top. Several gusts of a fluky southerly breeze blew the willows about, and many of their leaves fell quite heavily onto the water. For a moment, I wondered if the fish was ignoring me because it had grown to expect some commotion on such a day, but then decided that more likely its gaze was focused firmly on the bottom.

Trout like this 2.3 kg brown use undercut banks for shelter in shallow, silty waters like those of O'Dells Lake in background.

If so, what might be on its menu, and what fly should I change to? A particularly clumsy cast had finally sunk the Red Tag, and as I drew it back through the water, the trout bow-waved after it- but, as is usually the case, did not take. I stopped the retrieve, the Tag bobbed back to the surface, and the trout gulped at it! I struck with my usual speed, felt nothing and though flustered, put this down to the fish's rejection of the fly at the very last moment. Another dry might be worth a try, especially as a beetle or nymph fished wet in such shallow water would probably stir up the bottom too much.

farther than those made by the raindrops and, though just fractionally more pronounced, were quite obvious. I could still pinpoint its position-and perhaps, with the light now even dimmer, the fish might happen to look up, or at least around.

With the rain easing, that little fawn wing came down on the dark water again, but this time it went under in a silvery little bulge, up came the rod and the trout was on, at last. The battle was short but brisk, so brisk that I had to give line on several occasions, and at one stage was somewhat disconcerted by a cracking in the willows overhead caused by a possum on the move, perhaps also

Feeding trout often lie over this shallow glide on the Break O'Day River but for shelter just below is a large, deep hole.

So on went a size 15 Alder-if not taken for a beetle, it could represent a small dun. If not taken for either, with luck it might still look 'buggy' enough to eat. I finally managed to knot the Alder on after cutting the main tippet strand in mistake for the tag end at the irritating end of my first attempt in the gloom. At least half an hour had passed on this little billabong, the rain had at last begun to fall and the cold water trickling down my neck didn't do anything to improve my temper.

Heavy raindrops pock-marked the smooth surface and the trout continued to swirl, although nowhere near as busily. The rings it made extended

upset by the rain. But in the finish, that fish lay flapping on the silt a step or two away.

It wasn't quite the finish though, because the Alder unexpectedly flew up into the air-to leave the fish lying exhausted on its side, unaware that it was free. Careless now of any fuss I might cause, I waded as nimbly as I could to the trout, got a hand under it and scooped it up onto the bank. While certainly not a large fish, it wasn't a tiddler either, was in top condition and had been feeding on earthworms seasoned with the small, pale grubs which may have been beetle larvae.

Back at the bridge pool, I did make a show of

The small billabong beside the North Esk River where the trout described was caught.

casting to a couple of bulges in the deep, dark water under the willows and was not surprised at the lack of response, nor disappointed-success with that trout supping in its little billabong had already made my day.

As well as willows, native trees and bushes shade other lowland streams and ancient little pencil pines are appreciated by the trout in many of the thousands of lagoons and tarns which make up the western lakes on the Plateau. With no eyelids and with eyes having pupils fixed in diameter which, unlike human eyes, cannot close up or dilate to match the varying intensity of natural light, trout find comfort on bright days in the shade which also helps hide them by breaking up the outline of their shadows on the bottom.

Cloud cover reducing light intensity may encourage trout to feed actively. When food is about in quantity, on a day of patchy but dense cloud with periods of sunshine haphazardly alternating with dullness and with light varying constantly in intensity, fish will at times feed hard and perhaps because their vision is somewhat confused, without much of their customary caution. Such days can be red-letter occasions for anglers.

In some of the very open, shallow western lakes such as Lake Botsford, there are few undercut banks and little vegetation of substance in or around the water. On bright days there, noted local angler Allan Miller has marvelled at seeing trout suspended motionless, tails pointing to the sun and heads downward, probably using in desperation the meagre shade of their own bodies to shelter their eyes.

Trout in the smaller rivers look for shade not only from bankside vegetation but also, as in Little Pine Lagoon, among weeds growing in deeper gutters and channels. As well as food in the shape of careless terrestrial creatures, higher banks along these streams also provide shade. Patches of foam, perhaps where a wind lane on a lake ends against a dam, perhaps on the back eddy of a slow lowland pool or along the edge of quiet water bordering a strong corner current, often have trout under them hiding from the sun as well as predators.

Too much silt in suspension, caused in shallow stillwaters by wave action and in rivers by floods, will not only reduce a trout's vision but also hamper its respiration. As mentioned in the previous chapter, fish look for respite in clearer river backwaters and their like, and in various parts of lagoons. On the larger lakes, a good place for anglers to check is along the edge where muddy water meets the clearer main lake.

Where they have the choice trout prefer running water to still, but although a muscular and streamlined fish like a trout has a good shape to resist the flow, if it is too strong too much energy will be used up in holding position, and shelter is needed. During floods, fish seek shelter from the turbulent currents associated with them. Quieter backwaters, sidewaters, marshes and ditches become popular with trout which may travel along a well-defined watercourse up to a kilometre from the main channel. If they have sufficient water, food and shelter there, they may take up residence when the flood subsides.

In streams where faster flow is the norm, trout will favour the deeper, slower pools, especially if they are also sheltered from wind, but elsewhere a fish will look for a pocket of slower water, preferably close to the current which is bringing food to it. Little indentations making baylets in banks are favoured, especially if they make basins as well. So are rocks of various sizes along edges and anywhere across streams, either reaching through the surface, or submerged. Humps and bulges in the flow indicate where these are and where trout may well be holding, near the bottom in the slower water behind and among them. Heavy lures and fast sinking lines cast with sufficient slackness are needed to get down to these fish if they won't rise.

Rocks protruding above water will have trout resting behind some of them and, if they are large enough, occasionally in front. A lure such as a dry fly tied with buoyancy and high visibility in mind needs to be cast, not to a pocket of the slower water where it will quickly drag, but on the current close to either side of it where a fish will be watching for food coming down.

As well as shelter from predators, sun and current, trout comfort is linked very closely with the temperature of the water in which it lives. Temperature, which also affects the amount of oxygen dissolved as a gas in the water, is one of the most influential factors affecting the location of trout. Even though trout look for shade and water which is pure and preferably flowing, they seek, above all of these, water which is of a suitable temperature.

The actual time it was caught, with rain threatening to disguise its swirls.

Chapter 8

Trout Comfort - Temperature & Oxygen

Brown trout find very comfortable temperatures between 12 degrees and 20 degrees Celsius and often feed best at the top end of this range, while the preferred range for brook and rainbow trout is several degrees less. Trout are basically fish of cold water: rainbows can live for only limited

When a place like the Lily Pond at Arthurs Lake is shallow, trout cruise in channels such as the one just beyond the rocks.

periods in water temperatures of 28°C or more and the upper limit for browns is a degree less. But they can tolerate without problems temperatures just above freezing to lengthy periods in water up to 24°C, so long as temperatures do not change too abruptly.

Being cold-blooded, all fish have a body

temperature the same as the water which surrounds them. As it changes, so does the internal physiology of the fish, which just for this purpose is more loosely organised and flexible than that of a warm-blooded animal and provides a better buffer against external change. Enzymes which work best in one temperature range are replaced by others working best in the new range, but this does take time. Generally, temperatures should not change more than 5°C in a day, or 3°C when near the extremes of temperature which a particular species can stand. Furthermore, after such a change, the new temperature needs to be maintained for several days so that the changed internal equilibrium can become established.

For trout, too much heat is usually the problem. The reverse applies, however, early in the season, which for most waters in Tasmania is towards the end of winter, for a few weeks on lowland rivers and for longer in the colder highland stillwaters. Although many Australian lakes are classified as 'warm monomictic'-meaning they form into different layers, or strata, only in warmer weather and have complete circulation of water through them in winter-early in the season layers of water of different temperatures may be a factor in some lakes with warmer water located well down near the bottom.

This is because water is heaviest at 4°C; it becomes lighter as it grows colder and moves towards the surface, where of course it may freeze. Because at about 4°C trout also start to show an interest in food, if a thermometer confirms that the water is warmer deeper, then

Water can be cooler where feeder streams enter larger rivers. Pictured is Tasmania's Nile, just above its junction with the South Esk River.

A common pattern of thermal stratification in Australian lakes and reservoirs. Redrawn and modified from Bayly & Williams (1973).

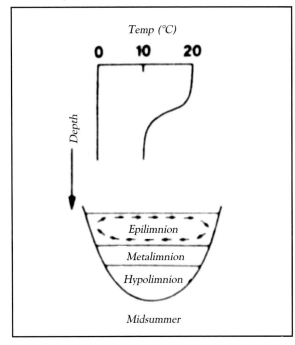

Temp (°C)

0   10   20

Depth

Epilimnion

Metalimnion

Hypolimnion

Midsummer

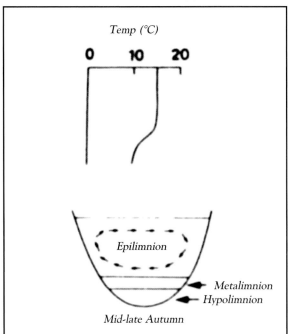

Temp (°C)

0   10   20

Epilimnion

Metalimnion
Hypolimnion

Mid-late Autumn

lures should obviously be fished down there. With waters like Little Pine Lagoon normally at a high level at the end of winter and fish busy down among the weedbeds searching for scud seasoned with a few snails, getting flies down to them may require a boat, or at least well-insulated waders.

Most Tasmanian lakes are shallow and, if they do stratify for more than a day, can be classified as 'polymictic'-stratifying for only some days throughout the year, rather than for full seasons over a yearly cycle as happens in the 'dimictic' lakes widespread in Europe and North America.

Any local lake ices over only in parts and for only a few days at a time, and more important on all Tasmanian lakes as spring progresses is the warmer surface water and the wind which blows it to windward shores, where fish tend to congregate in it.

In summer, larger, deeper lakes may stratify. The 'epilimnion', the upper of three layers, is less dense and is mixed by the wind to be uniformly warmer than the bottom layer, which is the 'hypolimnion' of colder, more stagnant water little affected by wind. The section in between is called the 'metalimnion' or 'thermocline', where temperatures drop rapidly as the depth increases, by definition falling by at least 1°C per metre.

With trout usually preferring the epilimnion, sometimes the metalimnion and rarely the

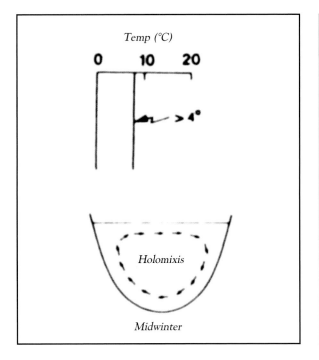

Temp (°C)

Holomixis

Midwinter

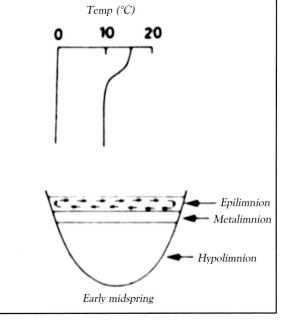

Temp (°C)

Epilimnion
Metalimnion

Hypolimnion

Early midspring

Aerial shot showing the course of the Little Pine River through what is now Little Pine Lagoon. As summer advances, trout seek cooler water in its depths.

hypolimnion, knowing where these are in various seasons is useful. In mid to late autumn, the ratio of epilimnion, metalimnion and hypolimnion by depth is 4 to 1 to 1-that is, the top layer comprises two thirds of the lake's depth. In winter there are no layers and in early to mid spring the ratio is 1:1:4. Nevertheless, it should be borne in mind that trout will tolerate deeper, colder water for short periods if that is where they need to feed.

Many of the main stillwaters, however, average only a few metres in depth and for the trout the discomfort of warm summer water is compounded by a double-barrelled problem. While warmer water holds less dissolved oxygen than colder water, it at the same time raises the metabolism of fish so that they need more oxygen and water has to be pumped through the gills faster. Active fish like trout, which normally live in cool and well oxygenated water, are particularly sensitive to reduced amounts of dissolved oxygen and this, combined with increased metabolism and their dislike for warmer water, ensures that trout will actively seek places where it is cooler.

On more confined areas of stillwaters on a hot Australian day, wind blowing warmer surface water to the far shore may cause a reverse current to develop in deeper water which may result in cooler water welling up along the other, lee shore.

Feeder streams can be cooler too, and trout numbers greater where they enter rivers or lakes. Other cooler places may be in the shade of vegetation and higher ground and in streams where springs add cooler water. Particular places where they well up from the bottom are known as spring holes and will nearly always be crowded by trout enjoying the coolness and increased supply of oxygen, which is also available to them in the faster runs where the rushing water enfolds it from the air.

This is illustrated by trout activity in the headwaters of north eastern Tasmania's little St Patricks River in summer. When water runs through its foothills thin, clear and warm, fishing in full daylight to risers in the slow, open, sunlit pools is often a waste of time, even though trout may remain on the fin delicately sipping tucker like tiny beetles and grubs drifting down. Far more productive when the sun shines overhead is faster, deeper and cooler water in narrow, well-shaded runs, where a Red Tag floater in sizes 14

to 16 is as good a fly as any.

In many if not most pools of the St Patricks near dark, however, you may cast small floaters as different as Red Tags and Hare's Ears, Royal Coachmen and Grey Dusters, wherever you please to fish splashing in water now cooler at small white caddis in the full expectation of a pleasant catch of small and bony, but firm and sweet elements for a pan-fried breakfast. Eating it early next day beside this river, to the music of birds and pure water, is another reason to esteem

how bracing the air here can often be at both ends of each day, even in summer.

Obviously, methodical use of a thermometer to find cooler water will result in better sport, which will usually remain better for season after season.

Deeper water is also cooler in summer. After fishing the summer dun hatches on Little Pine Lagoon intensively over many seasons, I find when wading that the weedy shallows about a metre deep are best fished during the first half of

With deeper water shaded and flowing briskly, this St. Patricks River pool remains productive during summer.

summer, but after that I favour shores where I can cast out over deeper basins and channels and especially over the course of the old river, in whose considerable depths trout seem to lie with gratifying consistency and in pleasing numbers. Furthermore, many larger, deeper stillwaters like Tasmania's Arthurs Lake contain extensive shallows, and anglers at places like Cowpaddock Bay, and the Lily Pond area of Tumbledown Bay to the north, usually find that basins, and especially channels among the weeds, are similarly productive in summer.

Shallow stillwaters may not only be too warm for fish but if they grow much vegetation may also contain too little dissolved oxygen because of the respiration of these aquatic plants. During the day, through the process of photosynthesis which involves sunlight, these plants produce useful oxygen but at night respire only and take it up. Dissolved oxygen levels in the shallows may be at their lowest early in the morning after a warm day of heavy overcast, which by reducing sunlight in turn limits photosynthesis and therefore the production of oxygen. If fish cannot move elsewhere, they may die.

Late in summer and on into autumn, the problem may be aggravated by plants beginning to die back and decompose. There may not be sufficient oxygen produced during the day to make up for the oxygen used at night through both respiration and decomposition.

Pollution levels also play a key role in the comfort of a trout, through its respiration rather than diet. The gill structure consists of a very fine, basket-like sieve through which water is pumped by the muscular action of the mouth and pharynx. This is done very efficiently by a trout, which can extract up to 80 per cent of the oxygen dissolved in the water, but this very efficiency also makes it vulnerable to poisons in the water.

The acidity or alkalinity of water, as measured on the pH scale with 'soft' acid water reading below the neutral 7.0 and 'hard' alkaline above, has an influence on trout, whose own blood is almost neutral at 7.1. They have problems with water registering below 5.0 or over 9.0 on the pH scale and seem to prefer a range of 6.8 to 7.8.

One reason for liking water slightly alkaline could be the competition that the calcium in hard water gives to heavy metals for uptake into trout at the surface of the gills. The toxicity of these metals is greatest in the soft, acid waters which unfortunately are common in mining areas where rain often leaches metals into water. This can go on from spoil heaps and tailing ponds long after mining has ceased, which probably accounts for why in eastern Tasmania the trout fishing for some kilometres of the South Esk River below Ormley has taken so long to recover from the discharge from Storeys Creek of water polluted by mining operations in the Rossarden area which ceased years ago. In a 1976 survey, no fish of any kind were found in the South Esk between Storeys Creek and a point 11 kilometres downstream! Good news in 1999 concerned action to remove contaminated waste rock from a dam on the banks of Storeys Creek and to divert acid drainage so that it could be properly treated elsewhere.

Obviously such pollution will affect where an angler looks for trout and so will the discharge of sewage effluent which, though seldom affecting the supply of food organisms, nevertheless poses a greater threat. This effluent contains organic chemicals which can be oxidised rapidly by bacteria and thus can reduce the concentration of dissolved oxygen to dangerous levels when it is not diluted enough in rivers and lakes, and especially when a heavy discharge occurs so suddenly that trout do not have time to acclimatise, or avoid it.

For the same reason, accidental discharges of farm wastes can also be hazardous, for example from silage and intensive livestock rearing. Effects on fish are worst where water is warmer: to less dissolved oxygen and increased fish metabolism is added an increased rate of bacterial decomposition which further increases the amount of carbon dioxide in the water, to a level which can suffocate fish.

For local anglers, nearly all central highland waters fortunately remain unpolluted, with the only occasional exceptions in the past being those beside major bushwalking tracks such as the Overland Track between Cradle Mountain and Lake St Clair, where careless disposal of human wastes has resulted in polluted drinking water.

More at risk are lowland streams like the Meander River, which flows through and near a number of towns and through settled farmland for much of its length. As for river basins anywhere, let's hope any increase in the number of residents is matched by sufficiently effective practices in treating their sewage.

Chapter 9

Finding Feeders - Other Factors

An image a good deal more exciting to the angler than the shiniest new sewage plant would be two kilograms of brown trout, tenuously attached to a small dry fly and sometimes in, sometimes clear of the crystal water of Lunka Lake. Just where to cast a fly on that isolated, pristine, placid western lake in Tasmania was decided partly on theory but much more by looking and taking into account the practicalities of the existing situation.

Big trout had been slashing at mayfly spinners as they hovered near the low bushes bordering the lake's outlet, a long, narrow arm which ranged downward almost at right angles to the southern shores of the lake.

But they did so only occasionally and without system, and a floater set out over several of them had been ignored. A light southerly breeze puffed at times directly up the arm towards the main lake, presumably taking with it any food on the surface. The mouth of the arm was only a couple of casts across, lying conveniently on its eastern side was a large flat rock to stand on, for a right-handed caster the breeze was no problem-and surely trout must be cruising in and out of this nice little bay?

And yet angling for trout remains much more of an art than a science: putting out that floating fly line and allowing it and the dry fly attached to curve slowly around with the breeze was still a small act of faith. When the take eventually came it seemed, like others before it, to be a wish wondrously come true... Nevertheless, anglers stand a good chance of enjoying similar sport fishing under similar circumstances across the mouths of other arms in other lakes.

The rapid rise of water levels can also result in excellent, localised sport and be a vital factor to consider in choosing where to fish. The flow of water through Bronte Lagoon, which power station operators normally allow to continue through their storage system, is sometimes blocked in summer so that it can be released a few days later for canoe competitions downstream. This results in a sudden rise in the level of Bronte which catches unawares juicy morsels like caterpillars, as does a summer flood on lowland rivers. In desperation many of them crawl up grass stems to escape, but most are overtaken sooner or later by the rising tide and float twitching and curling on it until accepted gratefully by cruising trout. As could be expected, anglers lucky or knowledgeable enough to be present usually enjoy superb dry fly sport, no matter how bad the weather may be.

Power station operators are also responsible for most of the sudden rises in level of tailwater fisheries such as Brumbys Creek. A re-regulation weir is to be built above Brumbys to dampen flows which will fluctuate more often when the Basslink scheme begins operating. Until then the water unexpectedly covering its silted, weedy flats will continue to hold trout following close behind to check on what manner of careless creatures may have been swept away, drowned or, like yabbies, caught out in the open by it.

Naturally, rain also boosts the level of Brumbys Creek, and when heavy and concentrated enough, it can raise abruptly not only streams but the smaller highland stillwaters as well. Although this may happen only a few times in a decade and the sport it caused may be cooled if snowmelt is combined with the rain, brilliant fly fishing like that described on Bronte Lagoon can be enjoyed by anglers on waters like Little Pine Lagoon and others of like size with similar flat, open, grassy surrounds.

Sudden high levels during times of flood are of course much more common on lowland streams. Thanks to the insights of vastly experienced anglers like David Scholes, locating trout feeding in them is now much more feasible and has already been

The same moon which makes discreet casting
difficult can yet be put to other uses by trouters-
especially as the river season closes tonight ...

Dramatic sunset on Macquarie River, Tasmania

mentioned in some detail earlier in this book: as along newly flooded lake margins, trout can be expected in still water up to a metre deep covering a bottom where prey can readily be seen. As David goes on to point out, however, because prey during a summer flood is more likely to resemble the caterpillars of Bronte Lagoon and their like, a dry fly can often be put to trout cruising over newly covered ground, which is usually so well covered by vegetation that the fish are looking upward rather than down anyway.

Nonetheless, with summer flood waters in streams often clear enough to spot cruising trout through polarised lenses, when their beat is fixed lightly weighted bait like grasshoppers, grubs and worms can be set out in ambush as well as dry flies. Boosted summer flows sharpen a trout's appetite while providing extra food to satisfy it, so spotting rises in levels by keeping an eye on river gauges, with many heights now shown on the Internet if not in newspapers, can result in memorable sport.

Good locations to find such sport are on rivers like the lower South Esk in northern Tasmania, fringed along many stretches by extensive networks of hollows, sidewaters and billabongs into which rising water easily spills. Summer wind becomes less of a problem too along the many short stretches where these are sheltered from it, and anglers can enjoy top sport even in a strong blow by regularly 'doing the rounds' of only three or four such places.

Sudden falls in levels can upset trout in some waters. While fish in Brumbys seem so accustomed to them that they retreat as a matter of routine to deeper water and continue feeding, on the other hand local anglers feel that fish in Bronte Lagoon are put off and sulk for a while.

Low water does allow anglers to get closer to fish feeding in weed in places like Lake Rowallan, a reliable water to try if low late in the season when aquatic bugs also interest fish. Low water also gives anglers a chance to study the contours and vegetation on the bottom of stillwaters, as well as currents in streams, and to find out why trout choose to lie in particular spots in them. Perhaps a boulder or log previously unknown may lie revealed or, as in one 'hotspot' on the lower Macquarie River, an unsuspected, deep, weedy little basin, normally with a nice flow along its ceiling and on its bottom the remains of an ancient little tree, long gone except for its roots digging like scabby old fingers into the mud.

When a trout finds such a suitable lie, its strong territorial imperative is reinforced by the obvious advantages and it will waste no time in returning when the water rises. This territorial imperative extends in part to favoured beats in stillwater: elongated circuits covering perhaps a hundred or so metres of shoreline, around which trout systematically and repeatedly cruise looking for food like scud. Recent research by one scientist suggests that in some stillwaters these beats are more favoured than previously thought and trout will frequently return to them. Even these trout, however, may often be influenced more strongly by the other factors mentioned in this book than by considerations of territory.

Certainly fish in other stillwaters seem to be for most of the time.

When moving about, trout may at times behave like sheep and cattle, and humans for that matter, by following a clearly marked track to save themselves the trouble of deciding where to go. While the importance of natural channels has already been mentioned, trout sometimes also seem to use as pathways drowned tracks actually made by stock, and by vehicles. A once-popular fishery where this seemed to happen in the recent past was Lake Sorell, especially in its extensive marshes when they were well covered by water.

Certainly more than a matter of habit for trout is the urge to spawn. Because trout are considered by many people to be poor eating at this time, because the fish themselves cut back on their feeding and there is little food available to them anyway and especially since the aim in Tasmania is to allow them to reproduce without hindrance by closing to angling practically all the waters involved, spawning is not the factor in locating fish that it is at fisheries such as Lake Taupo in New Zealand. There, big rainbow trout running to spawn up rivers like the famed Tongariro sometimes may be persuaded to accept a lure.

Rainbows not quite so challenging are to be found more mundanely by checking for escapees in streams connected to trout farms, such as at Brumbys Creek below the bottom weir, or in salt water as in Macquarie Harbour where farm cages are situated. There, in some estuaries south of Hobart and occasionally in the Tamar River, escaped Atlantic salmon may also be caught. Hydro power station outlets, for example where the water from the Trevallyn Dam discharges into the upper Tamar River in Launceston, may attract trout and other species feeding on fish chopped up by the turbines, as well as on whitebait.

To close on notes more rhapsodical and whimsical, trout will usually not be found feeding at night or in times of low light if anglers have a brightly shining moon behind their casting arms. If no shadows are thrown by trees or hills onto the water, and if the sky is cloudless, anglers could with advantage retreat and perhaps make use of the moonlight for other pursuits.

Trout will often be found feeding close to civilisation in places so convenient that anglers rushing farther afield would consider them fished out, if they gave them any thought at all. So

Flooded stillwater margins: like river trout, lake trout look for prey easily-spotted on a bottom like this when under a metre of water.

Lunka Lake: isolated, pristine, placid western lake on Tasmania's Central Plateau

common is this attitude that these places are often highly productive and the lone angler muttering about grass being greener can enjoy piquant success as trout come to net from stillwaters like Arthurs' Pumphouse Bay, or from rivers like the Derwent, and the South Esk at the Longford picnic grounds, under the noses of colleagues en route to and focused on places far more distant.

Finally, and fortunately, trout may ignore all of the principles outlined in this book. Like gold, trout may be where you find them and like gold they are to be treasured wherever that may be.

Bibliography

Buckney, R.T. & Tyler, P.A. (1973). 'Chemistry of Tasmanian Inland Waters'. *Internationale Revue ges Hydrobiologie und Hydrographie 58.*

Cole, G.A. (1975) *Textbook of Limnology.* St Louis: Mosby.

Fulton, W. (1990) *Tasmanian Freshwater Fishes.* Hobart: University of Tasmania and Inland Fisheries Commission of Tasmania.

Heacox, C.E. (1974) *The Compleat Brown Trout.* New York: Winchester Press.

Lloyd, R. (1992) *Pollution and Freshwater Fish.* Oxford: Fishing News.

Martin, A.A. and Littlejohn, M.J. (1982) *Tasmanian Amphibians.* Hobart: University of Tasmania.

McDowall, R.M. (ed.) (1980) *Freshwater Fishes of South Eastern Australia.* A.H. and A.W. Reed, Sydney.

NSR Environmental Consultants (2001, 2002). Basslink Impact Statements. Melbourne: Basslink.

Peterson, J.A. and Missen, J.E. (1970) 'Morphometric Analysis of Tasmanian Freshwater Bodies.' *Australian Society for Limnology, Spec. Pub. No. 4.*

Scholes, D. (1961) *Fly-fisher in Tasmania.* Melbourne University Press, Parkville, Victoria.

Sloane, R. (1983) *The Truth About Trout.* Tas-Trout Publications, Rosny Park, Tasmania.
————— (1989) *More About Trout.* Tas-Trout Publications, Rosny Park, Tasmania.

Smith, B.J. and Kershaw, R.C. (1981) *Tasmanian Land and Freshwater Molluscs.* University of Tasmania, Hobart, Tasmania.

Sosin, M. and Clark, J. (1976) *Through the Fish's Eye.* Andre Deutsch, London, UK.

Tasmanian Inland Fisheries Commission (1971-1995). *Newsletter.* Hobart: IFC.
—————(1996-). *On The Rise.* Hobart: IFS.

Tasmanian Parks and Wildlife Service (2001). *Frogs of Tasmania* (poster). Hobart: TPWS.

Williams, W.D. (1980) *Australian Freshwater Life.* Macmillan Australia, South Melbourne.

Index

Index